AUTHORITARIANISM

WHAT EVERYONE NEEDS TO KNOW®

AUTHORITARIANISM

WHAT EVERYONE NEEDS TO KNOW®

ERICA FRANTZ

OXFORD
UNIVERSITY PRESS

Oxford University Press is a department of the University of Oxford. It furthers
the University's objective of excellence in research, scholarship, and education
by publishing worldwide. Oxford is a registered trade mark of Oxford University
Press in the UK and certain other countries.

"What Everyone Needs to Know" is a registered trademark of
Oxford University Press.

Published in the United States of America by Oxford University Press
198 Madison Avenue, New York, NY 10016, United States of America.

CIP data is on file at the Library of Congress
ISBN 978–0–19–088020–0 (pbk.)
ISBN 978–0–19–088019–4 (hbk.)

1 3 5 7 9 8 6 4 2

Paperback printed by Sheridan Books, Inc., United States of America
Hardback printed by Bridgeport National Bindery, Inc., United States of America

CONTENTS

9 Conclusion   148

AUTHORITARIANISM

WHAT EVERYONE NEEDS TO KNOW®

1

INTRODUCTION

What Is the Purpose of This Book?

Stereotypes about authoritarian regimes are common. In the classic version, an authoritarian regime is a brutally repressive regime in which power lies in the hands of a single, eccentric individual. In some instances, this is an accurate depiction, such as in Uganda under Idi Amin or Iraq under Saddam Hussein. And it is one that is reinforced by stories in the news media of notorious dictators, such as Turkmenistan's Saparmurat Niyazov, whose annoyance with beards, lip syncing, and gold teeth prompted him to outlaw all three, with spiritual musing, the Ruhnama, becoming required reading to pass a driving test; or Libya's Muammar Gaddafi, who once stated, "Execution is the fate of anyone who forms a political party."[1]

But in many instances, this portrait of authoritarianism is inconsistent with the political reality. Take Singapore under the People's Action Party. Despite constraints on a number of political freedoms, there is considerable political pluralism in Singapore. Opposition parties are able to compete in elections and win representation. The leadership cannot act alone; it is accountable to the party elite, which also controls leadership succession.[2]

In other words, though some authoritarian regimes fit the classic stereotype, many others challenge common perceptions of what authoritarian rule looks like. Kim Jong Un of North Korea may dominate news headlines more than John Magufuli of Tanzania, but both men govern authoritarian regimes.

The purpose of this book is to dispel stereotypes such as these and provide readers with a sharper understanding of authoritarian politics. Drawing from theoretical and empirical studies on authoritarian rule, this book offers readers clear and accessible answers to the most important questions about authoritarianism. It synthesizes cutting-edge research on authoritarian politics in a manner that is easily interpretable to readers, giving them a broad overview of the major ideas, insights, and debates in the field of authoritarian politics and making clear why they matter. It supplements these discussions with real-world examples from around the globe to help bring theory to reality.

Ultimately, this book provides readers with a context for making sense of current and recent political developments worldwide and interpreting how they fit with what we know about contemporary authoritarianism.

Why Does Authoritarianism Matter?

In today's global political climate, better understanding authoritarianism is of renewed importance. After decades of decline, authoritarianism appears to be on the rise. In 2017, the watchdog organization Freedom House reported for the eleventh year in a row that political rights and civil liberties worldwide had decreased.[3] In recent years, democratic principles have eroded in countries as wide ranging as Thailand, Mali, Turkey, Hungary, and Ecuador.

This trend represents a marked departure from the general pattern of regime diffusion seen in the past few decades. With the fizzling of the Cold War, the proportion of democratic states in the world rose sharply, from 25 percent in 1979 to 60 percent in 2014.[4] Between the 1970s and 1990s, authoritarian regimes around the globe—including in many parts of Latin America,

Southern and Eastern Europe, and East Asia—collapsed like dominoes. And in recent years, a number of countries with long-standing authoritarian regimes, such as Burkina Faso, Tunisia, and Kyrgyzstan, have seen democratic gains. Yet, despite these developments and the optimistic expectations of modernization theory and the "third wave" of democratization (explained in Chapter 3), authoritarian regimes still dot much of the world's political landscape. In addition, though democracies currently outnumber their authoritarian counterparts, current trends are set to reverse this should they continue. This spells trouble for the international community on a number of fronts: democracy is correlated with lower levels of repression, declining poverty rates, and fewer inter- and intrastate wars, among other normatively desirable outcomes.[5]

The prevalence and persistence of authoritarianism underscore the importance of better understanding how politics works in authoritarian regimes, including who the key actors are operating within them, how they come to power, the strategies they use to survive, and how they fall. Such an understanding, in turn, paves the way for the development of more informed foreign policy approaches when dealing with authoritarian regimes, as well as more precise, empirically based analyses and assessments of their current and future actions.

What Are the Challenges in Understanding Authoritarian Politics?

Compared to democracies, we know very little about how politics works in authoritarian regimes. In the past, this was at least partially due to an underemphasis in the social science literature on authoritarian politics.[6] Yet, while scholars have historically devoted less attention to studying authoritarian regimes than democracies, this has changed in recent years. In the last decade or so in particular, research devoted to authoritarian politics has expanded dramatically,[7] likely because of awareness that authoritarian regimes are not going away any time soon. After all, authoritarian regimes still govern about a third of the world's countries today. And there are few indications that a major decline in authoritarianism is on the horizon.

Even with increased scholarly attention to authoritarian politics, however, our understanding of political dynamics in authoritarian regimes is likely to forever pale in comparison to what we know of behaviors in democracies. Authoritarian regimes are notoriously challenging to study. Internal politics in authoritarian contexts is often hidden from public view, the media are typically censored, reliable data hard to come by, and government-sponsored propaganda pervasive. Authoritarian regimes are difficult to study, in other words, precisely because they are authoritarian.

Take the example of Laos. Since 1975, the Lao People's Revolutionary Party (LPRP) has governed the country under one-party rule. Most major political decisions are made at the party congress, which is held every five years, and most political power lies in the hands of the LPRP Central Committee Executive Board. Beyond basic features of the Laotian political system such as these, however, many things about how politics works in Laos are unknown. The period leading up to the congress, for example, is one of "swirling rumour" due to the "excessive secrecy" that characterizes decision-making in Laos.[8] Observers are left guessing what is likely to come. Most can assess the types of individuals apt to wield political influence in Laos, at least on paper, but how negotiations take place and what the balance of power is like among key actors and institutions are often cloudy and up for interpretation. Political secrecy in Laos makes information hard to obtain, a problem the tightly controlled media exacerbates. Public criticism of the government in all forms is prohibited. In 2014, for example, the government made it a criminal offense to criticize the ruling party online.[9] The government owns most media outlets, and foreign journalists and international organizations must submit their reports to government officials for editing prior to publication.[10] Gaining insight into the specifics of how politics works in Laos is without question a difficult task and one that inevitably involves speculation.

Though Laos is an extreme example, in most authoritarian regimes informal guidelines drive everyday operating procedures.[11] This means that an examination of the written rules of the political game often reveals little about actual political practices, which are further obscured by the preference for secrecy over transparency.

For observers, this can generate challenges answering even the most basic political questions about politics in an authoritarian regime, such as who the de facto leader is and who has the power to challenge him. (The vast majority of dictators have been male.) As an example, most observers saw Prime Minister Vladimir Putin as the leader of Russia while Dmitry Medvedev was president from 2008 to 2012. Others challenged this assertion, however, pointing to Medvedev's efforts to assert his independence from Putin while in office. Supporting this, Medvedev stated in 2009, "I am the leader of this state, I am the head of this state, and the division of power is based on this."[12]

Making matters worse, the media typically face serious obstacles reporting on government behaviors in authoritarian regimes. The information that they do release is often biased and intentionally inaccurate, even about basic information such as economic growth rates. [13]

Contrast this with the reality in most democracies. The identity of the leader is usually fairly obvious. Even in democracies that are flawed, policymaking and leadership choice are generally transparent.[14] Both are typically the product of an observable process that follows clearly spelled out rules, occurring under the watchful eye of a relatively free media.

In sum, due to the very nature of authoritarian politics, authoritarian regimes create challenges for those interested in understanding them.

What Is an Authoritarian Regime?

There are a number of ways that scholars define an authoritarian regime. In this book, a *regime* is the "set of basic formal and informal rules that determine who influences the choice of leaders—including rules that identify the group from which leaders can be selected—and policies."[15] A regime is *authoritarian* if the executive achieved power through undemocratic means, that is, any means besides direct relatively free and fair elections (e.g., Cuba under the Castro brothers); or if the executive achieved power via free and fair elections, but later changed the rules such that subsequent electoral competition (whether legislative or executive) was limited (e.g., Turkey under Recep Erdogan).[16] In other words, in the operational definition of an authoritarian regime this book uses, the distinguishing factor separating authoritarian regimes from democratic ones is whether government selection occurs via free and fair elections.

This definition is minimalist. It does not integrate human rights violations or repressive acts, unless they pertain to the ability of the opposition to have a reasonable shot of competing in the electoral process. It says nothing about levels of wealth, economic openness, political stability, or state capacity.[17] This definition is consistent, however, with the bulk of mainstream research on authoritarian politics, where democracies are regimes in which "those who govern are selected through contested elections" and authoritarian regimes are "not democracies."[18]

Under this definition of an authoritarian regime, multiple leaders may come and go within the same authoritarian regime. China under the Chinese Communist Party exemplifies this well, as does Nicaragua under the Somoza family. At the same time, multiple authoritarian regimes may come and go within the same authoritarian *spell* (or span of years). The experience of Cuba illustrates this. Cuba has been authoritarian since 1952, but two distinct authoritarian regimes have led it during this time period: the first under Batista (in power from 1952 to 1959) and the second under Castro and later his brother (in power from 1959 to the present).[19] Chapter 2 discusses both of these distinctions and why they matter in greater detail.

Because definitions of authoritarian regimes occasionally differ across the literature, the book will make clear, where relevant, when specific theories conceive of authoritarianism differently and the impact such conceptualizations have on understandings of authoritarian politics.

How Have Conceptualizations of Authoritarian Regimes Changed throughout History?

Authoritarian regimes have existed for hundreds of years, as the pharaohs of ancient Egypt, the Emperors of Rome, and the absolute monarchs of Europe exemplify. Yet, today's authoritarian regimes have evolved considerably since their predecessors governed many centuries ago.

Early authoritarian regimes typically featured monarchs and chiefs as the sole individuals with power; concentration of authority was the norm and there were few efforts to pretend otherwise.[20] The goal was to demonstrate complete control, not hide it. Today's authoritarian regimes, by comparison, exhibit a fuller range of behaviors. In some power is highly concentrated in the hands of a single individual, while in others it is dispersed across an elite leadership group. Even in those instances in which there is one-man rule, today's authoritarian regimes often go to great lengths to conceal that they are authoritarian (a characteristic that is emphasized throughout this book). For example, though Jordan and Qatar today are monarchic dictatorships that use hereditary succession procedures for determining leadership, unlike the monarchic dictatorships of the past, they feature institutions that we typically associate with democracies, such as legislatures and elections.

Not surprisingly, how observers conceptualize authoritarian rule has changed in line with these developments. As an illustration, though many of today's definitions of an authoritarian regime emphasize how it differs from a democracy, only in the past few centuries has democracy as a form of government become popular and widespread. Because conceptualizations of authoritarianism have evolved in tandem with manifestations of authoritarianism, the two are referenced simultaneously here.

Research on early experiences with authoritarian rule is abundant. This discussion focuses on developments beginning around the turn of the twentieth century to narrow the lens.

In the first part of the 1900s, a crop of new democracies emerged on the global scene only to face serious challenges, such as Weimar Germany. These developments inspired theoretical work on authoritarian rule that was normative in nature, centering on an analysis of the "ideal" type of government. A number of scholars at this time promoted the benefits of oligarchic rule and questioned whether liberal democracy was possible. Indeed, though we often think of democracy as the preferred form of government, "before 1945 the very idea of liberal democracy was anathema."[21] Observers on both sides of the political spectrum criticized liberal democracy for its inability to address key social problems and the corruption of its politicians, among other issues.

Such critiques drew from the elite theorists of this era, such as Gaetano Mosca, Robert Michels, and Vilfredo Pareto, who proposed that oligarchic rule was the most feasible form of social and political organization.[22] They observed that every political system featured a small group of elite that dominated a large, disordered mass citizenry. According to this reasoning, the intellectual superiority of the elite coupled with the masses' disorganization meant that any concerted political action required elite governance. Carl Schmitt, for example, wrote in his seminal 1921 book *Dictatorship* that governments' need for extraordinary powers during times of emergency necessitated authoritarian rule.[23] Liberal democracy, in this view, is thus unfeasible. Emilio Rabasa advocated similar ideas in his analysis of Mexican politics and the authoritarian regimes of Benito Juarez and Porfirio Diaz, suggesting that periods of authoritarian rule are necessary precursors to liberal democracy.[24]

Subsequent global developments, however, transformed the types of authoritarian regimes in existence, and consequently how scholars thought about them. The aftermath of World War II led to the emergence of a new concept: totalitarianism. Drawing heavily from the experiences of a handful of notorious authoritarian regimes, namely Nazi Germany and the Soviet Union, research on totalitarianism identified a number of traits specific to these types of regimes. Hannah Arendt, for example, stated in her seminal work *The Origins of Totalitarianism* that totalitarian regimes were extreme forms of authoritarian rule in which the leadership exercised full control over "atomized, isolated individuals."[25] In such regimes, ideology was central to political power and—to perpetuate the illusion of an ideal society—government propaganda was widespread. Governments used these messages to fundamentally transform society in line with their vision and turned to terror to ensure compliance. Other scholars picked up on Arendt's themes, emphasizing the following key features as critical to totalitarianism: reliance on a single political party, the use of a highly developed regime ideology, and the maintenance of a powerful security apparatus.[26]

Totalitarianism started to lose its analytic appeal around the time of World War II, however, as new dictatorships emerged that did not fit the totalitarian mold. Though many Communist regimes in Eastern Europe and Asia exemplified the totalitarian model, for example, others behaved quite differently. Take Spain under Francisco Franco. The regime did not seek to fundamentally change society, nor did it rely heavily on ideology to maintain control; instead, the central goal was the depoliticization and demobilization of the masses. Scholars distinguished such regimes, which they referred to as "authoritarian," from their totalitarian counterparts based on the contrasting role of ideology and nature of citizen–regime relations. Before long, however, the emphasis on ideology as a means of differentiating authoritarian regimes waned, as well, and totalitarianism as a concept lost its analytical utility.[27]

World War II brought with it the collapse of many colonial empires. Many of the new authoritarian regimes that emerged at this time therefore came on the heels of the independence movements that swept across much of the developing world in the 1950s and 1960s. Opposition groups often used a political party as the vehicle to mobilize their supporters during the independence struggle, and—where authoritarian regimes were established afterward—the same political party frequently remained dominant. Examples include the Kenya African National Union, which governed Kenya following its independence in 1963, and the People's Action Party, which governed Singapore following its independence in 1965. Indeed, many of the authoritarian regimes that have emerged since World War II feature a dominant party, just as in Nazi Germany and the Soviet Union. Yet, they have been quite varied in terms of the extent to which they emphasize a specific ideology, societal transformation, or mass mobilization. These developments prompted new ways of thinking about dominant-party rule and efforts to classify it. Samuel P. Huntington and Clement H. Moore, for example, disaggregated dominant-party regimes based on the strength of the ruling party.[28] In strong dominant-party regimes, the party is supreme, whereas in weak dominant-party regimes, the leader or the military is. Analysis of the intensity and duration of the regime party's struggle to gain power helps account for these different paths.

Cold War geopolitical dynamics brought to power a number of military-led dictatorships in the 1970s, particularly in Latin America. A single man in uniform governed some of these regimes, such as in Uganda under Idi Amin. In others, the military as an institution took over the reins of power, such as in Brazil under its military junta. This led to analyses of particular features of military rule and attempts to distinguish such regimes. Amos Perlmutter, for example, split military dictatorships into two categories: ruler types, which seek to maximize power and view civilians as threatening to stability, and arbitrator types, which seek to restore order to the country and have little intention of governing for long periods of time.[29]

This era also saw the emergence of strongman rulers, particularly in sub-Saharan Africa. Examples include Mobutu Sese Seku's regime in what is now Democratic Republic of Congo (formerly Zaire) and Jean Bedel Bokassa's reign in the Central African Republic. These regimes feature a single leader at the helm unchecked by other actors, similar to the Latin American caudillos who governed much of that region many decades earlier. New research came to the fore to better understand these regimes, as well, such as Michael Bratton and Nicolas Van de Walle's work on neopatrimonial rule in sub-Saharan Africa.[30]

The end of the Cold War led to additional changes in the authoritarian landscape. International pressures for authoritarian regimes to pursue political reforms (often tied to foreign aid) prompted many to open up their political systems. Though a number of authoritarian regimes featured legislatures and multiparty electoral competition even before the Cold War's end, the percentage that did so increased substantially after 1990 (a subject discussed in more detail throughout this book). Today, dictatorships with pseudo-democratic institutions such as these are the norm. New research emerged concurrently to make sense of these developments, generating a variety of new terms to refer to them, including "hybrid," "gray-zone," "electoral authoritarian," and "competitive authoritarian" (explained in Chapter 5).

To summarize, authoritarian regimes have evolved considerably over time in response to historical events and global political undercurrents, as has how we conceptualize them.

Are Authoritarian Regimes, Dictatorships, and Autocracies the Same Thing?

In this book, yes. Though in the past, scholars made clear distinctions between the terms "authoritarian regime," "dictatorship," and "autocracy," contemporary research increasingly uses them interchangeably. This book will follow suit. In those instances in which specific studies make a point of differentiating these three terms, the discussion will be clear to indicate and explain this, but otherwise this book views them as one and the same.

If Governments Hold Regular Multiparty Elections, How Can They Still Be Authoritarian?

It is common to associate regularly held multiparty elections with democracy. After all, the defining feature of democracy is free and fair electoral competition. Not all electoral competition meets these requirements, however; simply holding a multiparty election by no means guarantees that the contest will be free and fair. A free election is one in which most of the adult population can vote; a fair election is one in which multiple parties are able to participate and compete on a relatively even playing field absent widespread fraud. If a government bars a certain sector of the population from voting, such as a specific ethnic group, the election is not democratic. Likewise, if a government bans a major political party from competing, jails its leaders, or stuffs the ballot box to ensure its own victory (to give but a few examples of what unfair means in practice), the election is not democratic. This means that it is very possible for multiparty elections to fall short of standards of freeness and fairness, and consequently very possible to have multiparty electoral contests occur in authoritarian contexts.

A multiparty election, therefore, tells us little regarding whether a country's political system is authoritarian or democratic. To make such an assessment requires many more details regarding the nature of the electoral race, as well as government behaviors leading up to and after it. For example, an election may appear competitive on election day, but conceal unfair activities that occurred prior, such as the incumbent prohibiting opposition parties from accessing the media. Likewise, incumbents may lose a competitive election, yet opt to annul the results and stay in office. Put simply, multiparty electoral competition does not imply democratic rule.

In fact, most contemporary dictatorships feature institutions that mimic democracy, such as elections with multiple political parties. Though such institutions are a defining feature of "hybrid," "gray-zone," "electoral authoritarian," and "competitive authoritarian" regimes (terms explained in Chapter 5), they are actually not unique to this subset of authoritarian systems.[31] In modern dictatorships, it is common to see multiparty elections that occur on a regular basis.

Most scholars agree that authoritarian regimes incorporate pseudo-democratic institutions for survival purposes.[32] Though the logic explained for this varies, the evidence suggests that dictatorships with multiple political parties, legislatures, regular elections, and so forth last longer in power than those without them (a subject taken up in further detail in Chapter 7).[33]

In conjunction with their survival benefits, post–Cold War geopolitical dynamics have also incentivized authoritarian regimes to adopt pseudo-democratic institutions, as referenced earlier. In 1970, for example, 59 percent of all dictatorships held regular elections with multiple political parties. As of 2008 (the most recent year for which there are data), 83 percent of all dictatorships do.[34] This indicates that the vast majority of today's dictatorships feature multiparty electoral competition.

What Time Period Does This Book Focus On?

This book is about contemporary authoritarianism. It therefore focuses primarily on authoritarian political dynamics from the post–World War II period to the present, consistent with most contemporary research on authoritarian politics. World War II triggered the collapse of many colonial empires and set in motion a string of independence movements worldwide. The number of countries in the world increased dramatically in the years that followed as a result, making World War II a reasonable starting point for analyzing contemporary authoritarianism.

Why Does This Book Emphasize Trends over Time in Authoritarian Politics?

Most of the research from which this book draws analyzes authoritarian politics in the post–World War II period, as explained earlier. And most of the central insights that surface from this research are applicable to the authoritarian regimes of today, as well as those of the 1940s and 1950s. For the most part, the same political actors that were important then are important now and their preferences now are the same as they were then.

That said, there are indications of changes in authoritarian political dynamics on a variety of fronts from the Cold War compared to after it. During the Cold War, many countries served as pawns in the strategic game the United States and Soviet Union were engaged in. Not only were many nudged (and in some cases coerced) into establishing an authoritarian system of government, but those authoritarian regimes that did exist often received financial and material backing to support their rule. In a number of instances, authoritarian regimes exploited these dynamics to their advantage, exaggerating the threat of Communism (or, conversely, overstating their commitment to it) as a means of increasing their bargaining leverage. After the Cold War's end, however, many of these geopolitical relationships unraveled. The dramatic withdrawal of external support exposed many authoritarian regimes to serious vulnerabilities, in turn setting the stage for a global wave of democratization (discussed in Chapter 3).

Since the end of the Cold War, the consensus to emerge in the international community is that democracy is the preferred form of government. As a consequence, countries often must demonstrate support for democratic norms and institutions in order to secure external financial and material assistance. Such pressures partially explain why we see so many authoritarian regimes today feature pseudo-democratic institutions, as discussed earlier.

These are but a few indicators of how the geopolitical landscape during the Cold War differed from the one that emerged after it in ways that significantly affected the nature of authoritarian politics.

For this reason, this book places special attention on trends in authoritarianism occurring over time. It makes a point, where relevant, to highlight how authoritarian political dynamics are different today than they were in the past and why such differences matter. Readers should therefore come away from the book with a solid understanding of how authoritarian politics works in the broad sense, as well as the nuanced ways in which it has changed and may continue to change down the road.

What Data Are Used to Measure Authoritarian Regimes in This Book?

This book presents basic statistics about authoritarian regimes, where relevant. These statistics draw from the Autocratic Regimes Data Set, unless otherwise noted.[35] The Autocratic Regimes Data Set measures the start and end dates of authoritarian regimes in countries with populations over one million. It also measures authoritarian regime type (whether personalist, military, dominant-party, or monarchic—categories discussed in greater detail in Chapter 5), how authoritarian regimes end, and whether democracies or new authoritarian regimes succeed them. The original data set covers the years 1946 to 2010. I updated a number of the variables in this data set through 2014. The authoritarian regime statistics offered in this book will therefore vary in the years they cover (either through 2010 or through 2014), depending on data availability. This will be noted, where relevant.

What Will You Read in the Chapters to Come?

The goal of this book is to give readers a clearer understanding of authoritarian politics. To do so, it will cover the basics of how politics works in authoritarian regimes and how this, in turn, affects key things that we care about.

Chapter 2 sets the stage for the subsequent chapters. It outlines who the key actors are in authoritarian regimes and defines their preferences and interests. It suggests that politics in authoritarian contexts typically centers on the interplay between three actors: leaders, elites, and the masses. Leaders and elites take part in a constant struggle for power, rooted in a desire for greater political influence, all while working to maintain the support of critical sectors of the masses. Authoritarian institutional environments (discussed in Chapter 5) shape how these struggles take place and their subsequent political outcomes. This chapter closes by explaining the importance of differentiating authoritarian leaders from authoritarian regimes as units of analysis. Though in some instances the leader and the regime are indistinguishable, in many others the regime lasts well beyond the tenure of any single leader. It also explains how authoritarian regimes differ from authoritarian spells and why this matters for analyzing authoritarian politics. Specifically, multiple authoritarian regimes can come and go during a single authoritarian spell. Nicaragua was authoritarian for the entire period between 1936 and 1979, yet experienced two distinct authoritarian regimes: the regime of the Somoza family from 1936 to 1979 and the regime of the

Sandinistas from 1979 to 1990. The chapter makes clear the implications of these and other distinctions.

Chapter 3 paints a portrait of the authoritarian landscape. It describes the relationship between economic conditions and political regime type and disentangles the causal mechanisms that link them. Just as modernization theorists observed many years ago, democracy and economic development seem to go together. Richer countries are more likely to be democratic, and poorer countries are more likely to be authoritarian. This chapter offers insight into why. It also explains what "waves" and "reverse waves" of democratization are and highlights when and why we have seen them. It closes by describing where we see authoritarian regimes today and how the geographical dispersion of authoritarian regimes has evolved since the end of World War II.

Chapter 4 narrows the focus to authoritarian leadership. All authoritarian leaders have the same goal: to stay in power for as long as possible. Because of this, most try to secure personal control over as many major political instruments as they can while in office, such as assignments to key posts, policy directives, and the security forces. Some are successful in their efforts to maximize power, such as Amin of Uganda, but many are not, such as Mahmoud Ahmadinejad of Iran. This chapter discusses the behaviors of authoritarian leaders, with a special emphasis on the process of personalization—or concentration of power in the hands of the leadership. It discusses the negative consequences of personalization for global democracy, economic prosperity, and other outcomes of interest; shows that personalization is on the rise worldwide in authoritarian contexts; and identifies clear warning signs that it is occurring. The chapter also offers basic information about how authoritarian leaders typically leave power, what happens to them once they do, and how fear of post-tenure punishment can provoke them to engage in aggressive and predatory behaviors.

Chapter 5 broadens the analysis to authoritarian regimes. Authoritarian regimes are not one and the same, as the stark contrast between places such as Mexico under the Institutional Revolutionary Party (PRI) and Nicaragua under the Somoza family makes clear. Differences among them help explain differences in their behaviors across a wide range of domains. Scholars have proposed a number of ways to categorize authoritarian regimes for this reason, which this chapter reviews. It discusses the advantages and disadvantages of the major contemporary typologies, being careful to differentiate continuous typologies (e.g., gray-zone regimes, hybrid regimes) that place authoritarian regimes along a linear spectrum ranging from authoritarian to democratic from categorical typologies (e.g., military regimes, monarchic regimes, party-based regimes) that place them into distinct categories regardless of how "authoritarian" they are. This discussion is intended to help readers make sense of what the variety of terms used in the media and elsewhere to categorize authoritarian regimes actually refer to. This chapter goes on to explain in detail one of the most commonly used typologies in the literature, which disaggregates authoritarian regimes based on whether they are ruled by a military, dominant political party, royal family, or single individual. It then shows the consequences of these differences for a variety of policy outcomes in international and domestic arenas.

Chapter 6 covers how authoritarian regimes gain power. Some authoritarian regimes seize control via coup, such as the Chilean regime under Agosto Pinochet that remained in power from 1973 to 1989. Other authoritarian regimes assume control in a subtler fashion via authoritarianization, such as the regime Hugo Chavez established in Venezuela in 2005 that is still in power at the time of writing. How an authoritarian regime gains power is important because it often sets the stage for how politics will work down the road, such as the role the military will play and the constraints the leader will face. This chapter discusses the major ways that new authoritarian regimes form. It makes clear how these modes of entry differ based on whether the outgoing regime is an authoritarian regime or a democracy. In light of the global trend of democratic backsliding in recent years, much of the chapter is devoted to the dismantling of democracies. It explains what backsliding is, how it is that we know it when we see it, and the types of democracies that are the most vulnerable. It also details the relationship between populism and backsliding, illustrating how populist rhetoric among democratically elected leaders can be a springboard for transitions to authoritarianism.

Chapter 7 delves into authoritarian strategies for survival. All governments face the challenge of how to hold on to office. This is particularly true for authoritarian governments, which confront the constant threat of ouster because they cannot rely on electoral legitimacy to defend their position. To address this challenge, authoritarian regimes have two broad tools at their disposal: repression and co-optation. Repression is a defining feature of authoritarianism. Unlike in democracies where governments that repress heavily can be voted out of office, in authoritarian regimes repressive acts often go unpunished. For this reason, authoritarian regimes are far more likely to rely on repression to maintain control than are their democratic counterparts. In addition to repression, authoritarian regimes often use co-optation. Patronage is one form of co-optation, but so is the establishment of institutions, such as political parties and legislatures. These institutions incorporate potential opponents into the regime apparatus, thereby reducing their incentives to seek the leader's overthrow. In devising their plan for survival, authoritarian governments weigh the costs and benefits of both tools. This chapter discusses repression and co-optation in detail, showing the ways in which they are used in authoritarian regimes and how their use varies across authoritarian contexts. It offers insight into how contemporary authoritarian regimes differ from those of the past in terms of how they repress and co-opt. Rather than using brute force and a narrow set of traditional tools of co-optation to maintain control, today's authoritarian regimes use strategies that are subtler, wider ranging, and seemingly more democratic in nature.

Chapter 8 looks at how authoritarian regimes leave power. Given the persistent centrality of authoritarian regimes to the foreign policy agendas of many of the world's states, understanding their specific vulnerabilities is of substantial importance. This chapter reviews the major ways in which authoritarian regimes collapse and what happens afterward. Though about half of the time democracies are formed, the other half of the time we see new authoritarian regimes instead. This chapter identifies the major triggers of authoritarian regime failure more generally, before narrowing the focus to the factors that increase the chance of democratization specifically. It also discusses what political liberalization refers to and how it differs from democratization. It emphasizes that many authoritarian regimes adopt the same institutions that we have historically viewed as quintessential hallmarks of democracies—including elections, parties, and legislatures—even though they have no intention of using them for democratic purposes. As a consequence, political liberalization in authoritarian regimes does not necessarily suggest a likely turn to democratization down the road.

Chapter 9 summarizes and reviews the major themes of the book, before turning to a discussion of the critical unanswered questions that remain and the road that lies ahead in better understanding contemporary authoritarianism.

2

UNDERSTANDING AUTHORITARIAN POLITICS

Who Are the Key Actors in Authoritarian Regimes?

Politics in authoritarian regimes typically centers on the interactions of three actors: the leader, elites, and the masses.

The leader is the individual in charge of the regime. The leader cannot maintain this position, however, without the support of others. In dictatorships, the individuals whose support the leader requires to stay in power are known as elites (often referred to in the collective as an elite coalition, support group, leadership group, or winning coalition). The term "elite" can mean many things, but in this context it refers specifically to an individual who is part of the leader's support group. The leader's tenure is contingent on the backing of this group. The exact number of elites needed for a leader to maintain power is unknown; it likely varies from one environment to the next. The masses are the ordinary citizens living in an authoritarian regime, at least some of whose support the regime requires to stay afloat.[1] As with elites, precisely how many citizens whose support a dictatorship needs to maintain power is unknown and likely conditional on circumstances.

In democracies, formal rules stipulate the powers delegated to major political actors and how these actors are selected and deposed. Importantly, these rules are usually followed in practice. As a result, it is typically fairly easy to identify who key political actors are as well as whose support they need to maintain power, as discussed in Chapter 1. The process of removing key political actors from power is generally clearly spelled out, giving observers insight into how one would play out.

In dictatorships, by contrast, basic features of the political system such as these are often unclear. Informal politics is the norm. Formal rules usually exist, but they often do not guide behaviors in practice. Many major decisions are made behind closed doors, making it difficult to recognize who key political actors are, precisely whose support they need to maintain their positions, and the protocols that are followed to select or remove them.

While identifying who the masses are is straightforward in dictatorships, identifying who elites are often amounts to a guessing game. Observers usually have a sense of the nature of the broader group from which elites are drawn (such as a specific political party or branch of the military) but know considerably less about precisely who these individuals are and how much influence they hold. Even identifying who the leader is can be challenging in dictatorships.

Take the example of Iran. Since the revolution in 1979, Iran's official leader has been the supreme leader. The first supreme leader, Ayatollah Ruhollah Khomeini, held this position until he died in 1989, after which the current supreme leader succeeded him, Ayatollah Ali Khamenei. Iran's political system features a popularly elected president, in addition to the supreme leadership post, though electoral contests in Iran fall short of international standards of free and fair.[2] During Khomeini's tenure, the lines of authority were clearly drawn, with power unmistakably lying in the hands of the supreme leadership. Since his death, however, these lines have become blurrier. At various junctures, particularly during Mahmoud Ahmadinejad's presidency from 2005 to 2013, observers of Iranian politics raised questions over whether the de facto leader was the supreme leader or the president, given that the president seemed to be the more powerful of the two.[3]

The nature of authoritarian rule can obscure lines of authority, so much that it can be difficult to identify basic things we would like to know about an authoritarian regime. Though we know that the leader, elites, and the masses are the three central actors in dictatorships in theory, we often do not know the identity of elites and even the leader in practice.

What Are the Major Goals of These Actors?

Leaders and elites in dictatorships want power and influence, just as they do in democracies. They are therefore engaged in a constant struggle for power, with each vying for greater political influence than the other. Not only do elites compete with the dictator, but they also compete with one another. Amid this cutthroat environment, leaders and elites have to secure and maintain the support of key segments of the masses, while ensuring that those who oppose them have not reached a critical size. What the masses want is more complicated, though it often boils down to the basics, such as whether they are better off today than they were yesterday. (Institutions work to shape these dynamics, a subject taken up in Chapter 5.)

The central motivation of authoritarian leaders is to stay in office. They resort to a variety of tactics to do so, including annulling elections, extending presidential term limits, and sidelining those who could seriously challenge them. Unlike democratic leaders, whose positions are protected by formal rules that make removing them before their time is up difficult, authoritarian leaders face a constant threat of overthrow, at the hands of both the elites and the masses.

Authoritarian leaders usually assess that the most imminent threat to their rule comes from elites. The group whose support they require to stay in office is, ironically, also the group they must fear most. After all, the main goal of elites is to maximize power. Elites vie with one another for the most political influence, while also scheming to find ways that they themselves could secure the leadership. For this reason, the elite coalition poses a serious threat to the tenures of leaders. Indeed, the vast majority of dictators have been toppled by internal coups as opposed to popular uprisings.[4] As Winston Churchill said many years ago, "Dictators ride to and fro upon tigers which they dare not dismount."

Examples of elites playing a critical role in ousting dictators abound. In Nigeria in 1975, members of the Supreme Military Council ousted General Yakubu Gowon because they felt he was not consulting with them sufficiently. In Argentina in 1981, junta members overthrew General Roberto Viola because he chose to include civilians in the cabinet and started talks with union leaders. And in Ghana in 1978, Frederick Akuffo arrested and replaced Ignatius Kutu Acheampong, following a decline in Acheampong's hold on power. Akuffo was Acheampong's chief of staff.

Elites are the main political rivals of dictators and, consequently, the main source of their insecurities. Leaders engage in a variety of tactics to mitigate the threat elites pose to their rule, discussed in Chapter 4.

Mass-led overthrows of authoritarian leaders have historically been far less common than elite-driven ousters. For this reason, leaders tend to prioritize minimizing the likelihood elites will overthrow them. Yet, mass uprisings are not unheard of, as the wave of revolutions during the Arab Spring in 2011 illustrates. Authoritarian leaders therefore cannot afford to totally ignore mass sentiments. Because mass-led overthrows of leaders usually take entire regimes down with them, elites cannot afford to ignore the masses either.

The goals of the masses are often diverse, but they typically center on basic needs, such as the desire for mouths to be fed, roofs to sleep under, and security. This is not to say that mass audiences in authoritarian regimes do not long for greater political rights, but simply that economic concerns often trump all others.

When assessing how to attract the support of mass audiences, leaders and elites are strategic. They do not need *all* members of the citizenry to like what they are doing, just key sectors. There will always be citizens who oppose them. Authoritarian regimes have a variety of tools at their disposal to silence and sideline such individuals (discussed in Chapter 7), as well as substantial resources to do so.

This is a brief and generalized summary of the goals of the major actors in authoritarian regimes. Not all authoritarian regimes will fit this mold, but it is a reasonably accurate portrayal of broad political dynamics in many of them.

What Is the Difference between an Authoritarian Leader and an Authoritarian Regime?

An authoritarian leader is the individual at the helm of the authoritarian regime. An authoritarian regime is a broader concept. As discussed in Chapter 1, it consists of the basic rules (whether formal and informal) that control leadership choice and policies.[5] Sometimes, the leader and regime are indistinguishable, such as in Iraq under Saddam Hussein. But other times multiple leaders come and go during the lifetime of a single regime, such as in the Soviet Union.

It is important to differentiate authoritarian leaders from authoritarian regimes for two reasons. First, assuming that authoritarian leaders are synonymous with the regimes they rule masks the enormous variation that exists in the nature of leader–elite relations in dictatorships. Though in some contexts the locus of power in the authoritarian regime is firmly in the hands of the leader, such as in Belarus under Alexander Lukashenko, in others leaders must share power with other members of the leadership group. In Vietnam, for example, General Secretary of the Communist Party Nguyen

Phu Trong exerts substantial influence over key choices, but members of the politburo still retain influence. To be clear, leaders nearly always wield disproportionately more power than elites do, but in some authoritarian environments this is more lopsided than in others. A focus on authoritarian leadership that ignores the broader concept of the authoritarian regime will miss these key variations.

Second, and in a somewhat similar vein, authoritarian regimes often last much longer than the tenure of any single leader. Despite this, observers often assume that the fall of the leader implies the fall of the regime. To be fair, there are a number of vivid examples that come to mind of a leader's ouster ushering in a fundamental change of regime. In Iran, widespread protests in 1979 led to the Shah's ouster. A group of Muslim clerics assumed control afterward, bringing to power a radically different group of elites and rules and norms for selecting leaders and policies. In Romania in 1989, security forces executed then-leader Nicolae Ceausescu, following weeks of unrest. This paved the way for democratic elections held the following year. In the first instance the leader's overthrow led to the establishment of a new authoritarian regime, while in the latter it led to democratization.

Despite these famous cases, only half of all authoritarian leadership transitions result in authoritarian regime change (a dynamic discussed in greater detail in Chapter 8). The rest of the time, the leader leaves power but the regime remains intact.[6] In Myanmar, for example, the military ousted General Saw Maung in 1992. General Than Shwe, also a military officer and member of the State Law and Order Restoration Council elite, replaced him soon thereafter. The same group of elites controlled Myanmar despite the leadership transition; there was no change in regime. Intraregime leadership changes, it turns out, are quite common.

The frequency with which authoritarian leaders leave power without destabilizing the regimes they once led suggests that conflating authoritarian leaders with authoritarian regimes has the potential to distort our understanding of authoritarian regime vulnerabilities. This is important because it suggests that international efforts to destabilize dictatorships, pressure them to democratize, or otherwise change their behavior that focus on the leader as the unit of analysis may fail to bring about the intended effects.

What Is the Difference between an Authoritarian Regime and an Authoritarian Spell?

Authoritarian regimes and authoritarian spells are also distinct units of analysis. An authoritarian spell is a single continuous span of authoritarian governance. Just as authoritarian leaders can rise and fall within the same authoritarian regime, authoritarian regimes can rise and fall within the same authoritarian spell.

As an example, Nicaragua experienced a single authoritarian spell from 1936 to 1979, meaning that it had an authoritarian political system throughout the entire period. During this time, however, there were two unique authoritarian regimes. The first was the regime of the Somoza family, which governed Nicaragua from 1936 to 1979. The Somozas (whether directly or informally) were in charge of allocating political posts, doling out state resources, and managing the security sector. The leadership group consisted of members of the family, as well as a selection of their allies. The Sandinista National Liberation Front (FSLN) toppled the Somoza regime in an uprising in 1979, the culmination of a guerilla war that it began in the 1960s. Once in power, the Sandinistas nationalized a number of industries and took control of most of the Somozas' property. Many erstwhile supporters of the Somoza regime went into exile, while supporters of the FSLN found themselves in positions of power. The top leaders of the FSLN became the top leaders of the regime. Though these two regimes in Nicaragua are different from each other, they occurred during the same authoritarian spell.

Sometimes authoritarian regimes and authoritarian spells coincide, as occurred in the case of Brazil from 1964 to 1985. A single authoritarian regime governed Brazil during this period, and the country was democratic both before and after it. Often, however, multiple authoritarian regimes come to and leave power during the same authoritarian spell, as in the example from Nicaragua.

Authoritarian spells begin when a country transitions to dictatorship from a period of some other form of rule, whether it be foreign occupation, democracy, or state failure. Authoritarian spells end when the opposite occurs. Most frequently, democratic rule precedes and follows authoritarian spells, as in Brazil.

Why does any of this matter? For one, conflating authoritarian regimes with authoritarian spells risks ignoring the frequency with which authoritarian regime transitions lead to new authoritarian regimes. Observers often assume, for example, that the collapse of an authoritarian regime implies that democracy will follow it. Yet, the data indicate that from 1946 to 2010, just under half of authoritarian regimes that fell from power transitioned to democracy (discussed in greater detail in Chapter 8). The other half saw a new authoritarian regime assume control, or, in a handful of instances, the collapse of the state itself.

These statistics have clear foreign policy implications. Policymakers pursuing instruments designed to make an authoritarian regime vulnerable to overthrow should bear in mind the high likelihood with which such an overthrow will simply bring to power a new authoritarian regime (or, even worse, the state's dissolution).

It is possible, of course, that the new authoritarian regime will be more benign than its predecessor. In Chad, Hissene Habre's regime governed from 1982 to 1990. During that time, the regime was responsible for atrocities against citizens so serious that in 2016 an African Union–backed court in Senegal convicted Habre of ordering the killing of 40,000 people.[7] The authoritarian regime of General Idriss Deby, which came to power following Habre's ouster in 1990, is a far cry from "benign." Human rights violations, nonetheless, are not as severe as they were under Habre.

More frequently, however, new authoritarian regimes simply lead to new manifestations of bad behavior. The Democratic Republic of Congo offers an example. When rebel forces led by Laurent Kabila ousted Mobutu Sese Seku in 1997, the country (then called Zaire) was in shambles. Besides committing widespread human rights violations, Mobutu single-handedly destroyed the country's economy, all while amassing staggering sums of personal wealth. The Kabila regime (under Laurent and subsequently his son Joseph) has been no better, however. Human rights violations continue to be extensive, and economic problems remain serious. The Democratic Republic of Congo's Gross National Income (GNI) per capita, for example, decreased by 46 percent from 1990 to 2015.[8]

And, of course, there are plenty of examples of things getting quite a bit worse under new authoritarian regimes. The authoritarian regime led by General Omar Torrijos in Panama, for example, was substantially less brutal than the regime that succeeded it led by General Manuel Noriega.[9] Torrijos was fairly popular while in power, prompting many observers to refer to him as a "benevolent dictator."[10] This is in sharp contrast to Noriega, who was notoriously brutal and corrupt, prompting retired U.S. General and former Secretary of State Colin Powell to describe him as "pure evil."[11]

As an extreme illustration, the overthrow of the regime of Lon Nol in Cambodia in 1975 brought to power a new authoritarian regime led by Pol Pot, under whose rule nearly two million Cambodians died. Perhaps, as the saying goes, better the devil you know than the devil you don't.

These examples illustrate an additional reason why it is important to distinguish authoritarian regimes from authoritarian spells. Each authoritarian regime consists of a unique set of actors with distinct interests and norms of behavior. The theocracy of Iran has little in common with the Shah's regime that preceded it, for example. Using a spell as the unit of analysis in the case of Iran risks distorting our understanding of how authoritarianism works there. Spells can tell us quite a bit about a country's experience with authoritarian rule, but at the expense of lumping together very different modes of authoritarian behavior.

3

THE AUTHORITARIAN LANDSCAPE

Where Are We Most Likely to See Authoritarian Regimes?

Since the end of World War II, we typically have seen authoritarian regimes emerge in the developing world. This reflects the fact that level of development is one of the best predictors of authoritarian rule: as countries grow richer, they are less likely to be authoritarian. Beyond level of development, there are a number of other factors associated with authoritarianism, including: resource wealth (positively correlated), large Muslim populations (positively correlated), British colonial heritage (negatively correlated), and primary education attainment rates (negatively correlated).[1]

Establishing that these factors correlate with authoritarianism is fairly straightforward; determining that the relationship underlying them is causal, however, is significantly less so.[2] For many of the patterns we see, other explanations exist that could easily account for observed trends. In other words, though we have a good sense of the factors linked to authoritarianism, whether these relationships are causal or spurious is debated.

Causality aside, in the post–World War II era, there is a strong negative relationship between levels of wealth and authoritarianism: poor countries tend to be authoritarian and rich countries tend to be democratic. There are a few exceptions, of course. India, for example, was democratic long before its development boom in the last few decades. And many countries in the Middle East are both wealthy and authoritarian, such as Saudi Arabia and Singapore. That said, most of the time, authoritarian regimes govern in poor places and democracies in rich ones.

To illustrate this, Figure 3.1 offers boxplots with the distribution of level of development (measured using GDP per capita) in 2010, based on political system type.[3] The boxplots reveal that the median level of development (indicated by the line in the middle of the box) is much higher in democracies (at nearly $16,000) than it is in authoritarian regimes (at about $3,400). The lines around the boxes indicate the inter-quartile range, suggesting that most democracies have levels of development between $8,000 and $30,000, while most dictatorships have levels of development between $1,000 and $8,000. These represent sizable differences in per capita wealth across political system types. The dots in the plot represent outliers,

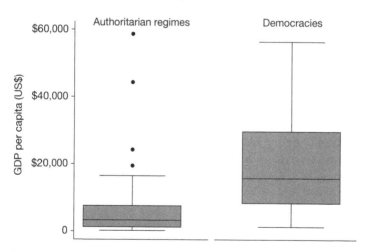

Figure 3.1 Level of development in 2010, by political system type.

highlighting the handful of dictatorship that buck the trend (in 2010, they were Kuwait, Singapore, Oman, and Saudi Arabia).

There are also clear patterns of regional clustering in the distribution of authoritarian regimes across the globe. Importantly, an authoritarian regime is likely to have authoritarian neighbors, and a democratic regime is likely to have democratic ones. Likewise, transitions to democracy as well as transitions to dictatorship appear to come in waves (discussed in more detail shortly), such that a transition in one country increases the chance of a similar transition in others nearby.[4] We do not necessarily know why these diffusion dynamics occur, but we do know that who your neighbors are matters.[5]

Why Are Authoritarian Regimes More Prominent in Poor Countries?

There is a strong negative relationship between level of development and authoritarianism, such that as countries grow richer, they are less likely to be authoritarian. Disagreement exists, however, regarding whether this relationship is causal, as referenced earlier. A vast body of research has examined this issue, and the jury is still out. This section surveys some of the key ideas and debates. Note that most of the research emphasizes the relationship between development and *democracy* (as opposed to its alternative, authoritarianism), so the discussion here will do the same.

In the 1950s and 1960s, modernization theorists were among the first to identify that development and democracy seemed to go together.[6] According to modernization theorists, as countries become more "modern," they become more likely to democratize; development in this view enables democracy.[7] The logic underlying modernization theory is that citizens in wealthier countries are more educated and urbanized, and therefore more tolerant and willing to compromise.

These qualities, in turn, are conducive to stable democracy. Some branches of modernization theory put the emphasis on class dynamics instead, arguing that increases in wealth lead to larger and more powerful middle classes, which provide the foundations necessary for dispersed political power.[8] Regardless, the central expectation of all modernization theorists—that such development *causes* democracy—is the same.

Down the road, however, scholars began to question the direction of the causal arrow in this relationship, suggesting that it could be democracy that causes development, as opposed to vice versa.[9] According to this logic, economic prosperity is only possible where policymakers are held accountable for their choices. If policymakers cannot be voted out of office as a consequence of bad decisions, they will opt to accumulate wealth in their own hands and destroy their economies. Democratic institutions, in this view, pave the way for economic development.

There are also a variety of indirect pathways through which democratic rule could raise levels of wealth. For example, democracies have better human rights records than dictatorships do, which may make their citizens more likely to invest in their economies.[10] Government violence against the citizenry, by contrast, may deter such investments. Democracies also spend more on public goods than dictatorships do and are known to devote greater resources to things such as public education, roads, and clean water.[11] Public goods, in turn, are shown to increase trade and human capital.[12] Democracies also have lower rates of corruption, which is harmful to economic prosperity.[13] And, perhaps as a consequence of all these factors, their citizens tend to live longer on average, and their infant mortality rates tend to be lower.[14]

The argument that democracy causes development is therefore plausible, but so is the argument that advocates the reverse. Unfortunately, disentangling the direction of the causal arrow has proven quite difficult.[15] Some studies find evidence of a relationship in one direction, others find evidence of a relationship in the other, and others find evidence of no causal relationship at all. For example, Adam Przeworski—whose work is among the most influential in this area—asserted in 2011, "I do not think that economic development necessarily leads to democracy but only that, once established, democracy survives in developed countries."[16]

The relationship between democracy and development is complex, and ascertaining whether there is a causal chain of events that underlies it is hard. Debates over why democracies are more prominent in rich countries and authoritarian regimes are more prominent in poor ones are therefore likely to remain unresolved for some time.

Why Are Some Rich Countries Authoritarian?

The negative correlation between authoritarianism and levels of wealth is fairly strong. That said, there are a few notable outliers, particularly authoritarian regimes that have been in power for decades in countries that are rich. Most of these rich authoritarian regimes are in the Middle East (with Singapore being a noteworthy exception). Examples include Qatar, the United Arab Emirates, Kuwait, and Bahrain.

Many of these outliers have a critical thing in common: natural resource wealth. Natural resource income, usually from oil, comprises a sizable portion of their economies. It is debatable, however, whether this is the reason they do not fit the trend. Though most countries that are rich *and* authoritarian have substantial natural resource wealth, this does not necessarily mean that they are authoritarian *because* they are rich in natural resources (a discussion that is expanded in Chapter 8). Authoritarianism took root in these countries at the time of independence for a number of historical reasons, most of which had little to do with natural resource abundance. In many, the same royal family that governed prior to independence simply stayed in power after it. Natural resource wealth therefore does not explain why they became authoritarian, but—by fostering regime stability more generally—it does help explain why they have remained that way since.

What Are Waves of Democratization?

Transitions to democracy often seem to occur in clusters. Take the collapse of Communism at the end of the Cold War. Less than a year after the fall of the Berlin Wall in 1989 that signaled the demise of the Communist regime in East Germany, long-standing Communist regimes in places such as Poland, Hungary, and Czechoslovakia fell from power, too. Waves of democratization, a term coined by Samuel Huntington,[17] refer precisely to these forms of clustered transitions to democracy.

When Have Waves of Democratization Occurred?

Following the end of the Cold War, Samuel Huntington famously identified three specific waves of democratization that had occurred up until that point in time.[18] The first was the "long" wave, which started in the 1820s and lasted for about a century. It brought 29 democracies to power, many of which formed following pressures to expand the suffrage to larger portions of the male population. The second wave of democratization occurred from 1943 to 1962. The key trigger of this wave was the struggle against fascism and the fall of colonial Africa. The third wave of democratization took place from 1974 to 2000. This wave began prior to the Cold War's end and includes the many democratic transitions that swept across Latin America in the 1980s, but really picked up momentum in the aftermath of the Soviet Union's collapse.

There were speculations about the advent of a fourth wave of democratization at the time of the Arab Spring in 2011.

Subsequent events, however, put to rest those conjectures, given that only Tunisia ended up democratizing.[19]

What Are Reverse Waves?

Transitions to dictatorships also seem to happen in clusters. In the early twentieth century, for example, authoritarian regimes overthrew democracies in Italy, Portugal, and Japan (to name a few) all around the same time period. Huntington refers to these clustered transitions from democracy to dictatorship as "reverse waves."[20]

When Have Reverse Waves Occurred?

There are two clear reverse waves that took place up until the end of the Cold War, occurring after the first and second waves of democratization, respectively.

According to Huntington, the rise to power of Benito Mussolini in Italy in 1922 set in motion the first reverse wave. By 1942, the number of democracies in the world decreased to 12, with Spain and Germany among the losses.[21] The second reverse wave took place between 1960 and 1975, bringing the number of democracies in the world from 36 (its peak after the second wave of democratization) down to 30. During this period, democracies fell in countries such as Lebanon, Turkey, and Greece, as well as throughout much of Latin America.

Huntington speculated about the possibility of a third reverse wave occurring following the end of the third wave of democratization. He suggested, writing in 1991, that such a development would be more likely should we see countries with weak democratic values, major economic crises, and social and political polarization, among other things.[22] Though there is little empirical evidence that these factors (apart from economic crises) systematically increase the chance of transitions to dictatorship, it is possible that we have witnessed a third reverse wave nonetheless. For example, though many countries

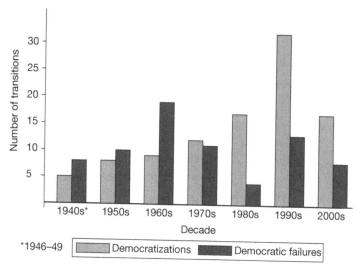

Figure 3.2 Transitions to and from democracy: 1946 to 2010.

in Central Asia never truly democratized following the collapse of the Soviet Union, there were moments of optimism that they would. Such hopes were dashed soon thereafter, however, as governments across the region increasingly governed with an iron fist.[23] For reasons such as this, observers debate whether a third reverse wave has occurred,[24] and perhaps only with the passage of time will we have a clear answer.

To illustrate some of these points, Figure 3.2 plots the number of transitions to and from democracy in the period 1946 to 2010. Consistent with Huntington's observations, it shows that the number of democratizations peaked in the 1990s, while the number of democratic failures was at its highest in the 1960s.

What Is the Authoritarian Landscape Like Today and How Has It Evolved?

From the end of World War II until the present, there have been substantial changes in the authoritarian landscape, both

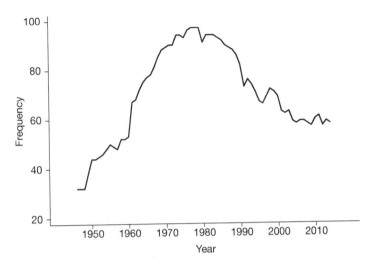

Figure 3.3 Number of authoritarian regimes in power: 1946 to 2014.

in terms of the number of authoritarian regimes in power in any given year and their distribution across the globe.

Figure 3.3, for example, shows the number of authoritarian regimes in power from 1946 to 2014. It reveals that authoritarianism in the world steadily increased from the end of World War II until around 1980. In the years 1946 to 1948, there were only 32 authoritarian regimes in power, the lowest number throughout the period. The number of dictatorships rose in the decades that followed, peaking in the years 1977 to 1979 at 97. This represents a sizable upsurge, and more than triple the number at the start of the period of analysis.

This may be due to the fact that there were simply fewer independent countries in the world in the 1940s than in the 1970s. With the fall of many colonial empires following World War II, newly independent countries formed all over the world in large numbers. In 1946, there were 63 countries in the world with populations over one million; by 1979, this number had skyrocketed to 130. Even so, if we look at percentages,

51 percent of the world's countries were authoritarian in 1946, but a whopping 75 percent were by 1979.

Cold War geopolitical dynamics more likely account for the rise in authoritarianism from the 1940s to the 1970s. Both the United States and Soviet Union devoted substantial financial, political, and military resources in support of authoritarianism during this time as a means of advancing their strategic interests.

The tail end of the Cold War saw a slow decline in the number of authoritarian regimes in power, such that by 1989 there were 86 authoritarian regimes in existence (representing 66 percent of the world's countries), a number that fell to 73 by 1991 (representing 57 percent of the world's countries) following the collapse of the Soviet Union. In the decade or so that followed, the number of authoritarian regimes in power continued this slow decline before leveling out in the mid-2000s. As of 2014, there were 59 authoritarian regimes in office, comprising roughly 40 percent of the world's countries.

These trends suggest that in terms of raw numbers there are more authoritarian regimes in power today than there were after the end of World War II. That said, the percentage of the world's countries authoritarian regimes govern is lower now than it was then.

Recent political developments worldwide suggest an uptick in authoritarianism is likely in the years to come, however. Though the data do not cover 2015 through the present, there are indications that democratic transitions to authoritarian regimes are outpacing authoritarian transitions to democracies.[25] For example, democracies in countries such as Nicaragua and the Philippines are on the cusp of dictatorship as of 2017, if they are not there already. Democracies appear on the verge of collapse in countries such as Hungary and Poland as well. It is, of course, possible that media headlines are more likely to center on democratic declines than on democratic gains—Burkina Faso's democratization in 2015, for example, seemed to occur without much fanfare. But the overall sense of many observers is that an increase in authoritarianism is occurring or at least on the horizon.

As an indicator of this, the watchdog organization Freedom House documented declines in political rights and civil liberties in 2016, titling its 2017 report "Populists and Autocrats: The Dual Threats to Global Democracy."[26] This marked the eleventh straight year it recorded a downward trend in global freedom. While these declines could simply be due to decreases in "levels" of democraticness rather than full transitions to authoritarianism, they are still suggestive of a potential reverse wave. Of course, this does not imply that we are going to see the sweeping reversions to dictatorship that occurred in the 1970s, but rather that we are likely to witness a modest resurgence of authoritarianism.

In terms of changes in *where* we have seen authoritarian regimes since the end of World War II, there have been important developments as well. In 1946, most of the world's dictatorships were clustered in Latin America (31 percent), Europe (25 percent), and the Middle East and North Africa (22 percent). At the peak of global authoritarianism, however, this regional distribution looked substantially different. In 1979, for example, 39 percent of the world's dictatorships were in sub-Saharan Africa, up from 9 percent in 1946. This sizable increase is likely due to the explosion of newly independent countries that formed in sub-Saharan Africa during this period of time. Twenty percent of the world's dictatorships were in Asia in 1979, up from 13 percent in 1946. This increase likely occurred for similar reasons. Latin America, Europe, and the Middle East and North Africa all saw increases in the number of dictatorships in power from 1946 to 1979, but decreases in the percentages they represented globally.

The end of the Cold War brought large changes to some regions and minimal changes to others. Not surprisingly, the collapse of Communism meant the dissolution of many authoritarian regimes in Europe, such that the percentage of dictatorships in the region declined from 9 percent in 1979 to just 3 percent in 1991 (with the number dropping from 9 to 2). Dramatic changes took place in Latin America during this time frame as well, and for similar reasons. In 1979, 17 percent of the world's authoritarian regimes existed in Latin America, but by 1991, only 7 percent did. The number of Latin American authoritarian regimes dove from 16 to 5. In Asia, the percentage of global dictatorships in power that came from this region remained about the same during this period (at around 20 percent), though the number in power declined from 19 to 14. Elsewhere, there were few changes in authoritarianism. In both the Middle East and North Africa and sub-Saharan Africa, the percentage of the world's dictatorships they housed increased from 1979 to 1991, but the number in power remained virtually unchanged. This suggests that the end of the Cold War had less of an impact on authoritarianism in those regions than elsewhere.

The regional distribution of authoritarianism looks fairly similar today to how it did in 1991. As of 2014, there were only two authoritarian regimes in Europe (Russia and Belarus) and only two in Latin America (Cuba and Venezuela), with each region accounting for just 3.5 percent of the world's dictatorships. About a fifth (22 percent) of the world's authoritarian regimes govern in the Middle East and North Africa. That region has seen few changes in authoritarianism since the peak of the Cold War: 15 dictatorships were in power there in 1979 and 13 remain in power as of 2014. Asia has seen a slight increase in authoritarianism. The number of dictatorships in power from 1991 to 2014 has risen (from 14 to 17), and the region now represents about a third (29 percent) of the world's dictatorships (up from 19 percent). These regimes are split fairly evenly across East Asia and Central Asia.

Sub-Saharan Africa is the exception. Unlike other parts of the world, there have been noteworthy changes in authoritarianism in this region since 1991. Whereas sub-Saharan Africa represented 52 percent of the world's dictatorships in 1991, this number decreased to 42 percent by 2014. This still means that more authoritarian regimes govern in sub-Saharan Africa than in any other region of the world (which is perhaps to be expected given its comparatively low levels of economic development), but the gap between sub-Saharan Africa and other regions of the world is narrowing. Moreover, the number of authoritarian regimes in power in sub-Saharan Africa has declined considerably since the end of the Cold War, dropping from 38 in 1991 to 25 in 2014.

To summarize, today most authoritarian regimes operate in sub-Saharan Africa, Asia, and the Middle East and North Africa. As of 2014, there were only four dictatorships in power outside of these three regions.

That said, aforementioned global developments give pause to assertions that some regions are immune to the onset of authoritarianism. Many of the democracies that currently appear to be on the verge of transitioning to dictatorship lie in Europe, for example. Should such transitions materialize in the coming years, they would challenge our understanding of the emergence of authoritarian rule, which we typically view as unlikely where levels of wealth are high.

4

AUTHORITARIAN LEADERSHIP

Why Study Authoritarian Leaders?

Authoritarian leaders operate at the helm of the authoritarian political system. They nearly always wield disproportionately more power than other domestic political actors do. In many ways, they function as a veto player: key decisions require their support, and major policies cannot get passed unless they agree to them.[1] If we want to understand political outcomes in authoritarian regimes, therefore, we need to look first to the preferences of the leaders who rule them.

We know that the unique personalities, backgrounds, and idiosyncrasies of authoritarian leaders can influence their political choices, as can those of democratic leaders. For example, Idi Amin of Uganda had little education and was effectively illiterate.[2] While in power from 1971 to 1979, he purged educated officials from positions of power and replaced them with inexperienced novices.[3] He was known to shun expert advice, preferring instead to rely on the insights of soothsayers and his own gut instincts.[4] Amin's lack of education may explain why he found educated individuals intimidating and threatening while in office. It is plausible, in other words, that his behaviors—which ultimately led to disastrous policy choices that destroyed the Ugandan economy and incited war with Tanzania—are related to his own personal background.

At the same time, it is difficult to establish this empirically.[5] How do we know that outcomes in Uganda would have been different had a different individual been in power? Counterfactual thinking can shed some light on questions such as this, but it is not always easy to effectively carry out in practice.[6]

Though it is tempting to point to idiosyncrasies of an individual leader as the cause of a specific outcome, the context and incentive structures they confront may matter more than we think.[7] In the case of Uganda, Amin ruled in an environment in which there were few real constraints on the leadership, as was the case with his predecessor, Milton Obote. Such constraint-free political atmospheres in authoritarian regimes typically see leaders purging challengers, favoring loyalty over competence in the selection of their advisors, and pursuing erratic policy choices.[8] Amin's behavior is therefore consistent with what we might expect given the structure of the system he governed in.

Without denying that a leader's unique personality, background, and quirks can influence political outcomes, this book emphasizes the ways in which incentives and constraints shape a leader's choices. The goal is to bring to the surface predictable trends in terms of the types of behaviors we might expect authoritarian leaders to exhibit based on context. This is critical for understanding authoritarian politics given that the leader's support is required for virtually all key policies in dictatorships.

Why Do Some Authoritarian Leaders Seem More Powerful Than Others?

In some authoritarian regimes, leaders are seemingly omnipotent, such as in North Korea under Kim Jong Un, whereas in others they seem perpetually in the middle of tense battles with opponents, such as in Venezuela under Nicolas Maduro. Such differences across authoritarian regimes in the power leaders wield vis-à-vis other regime actors are not due to differences in the desire of leaders to amass control, but instead in their ability to do so given the context they are governing in.

These observations stem from this book's underlying assumption that all authoritarian leaders seek to maximize their own political power. Their political choices will therefore reflect this quest for control. The ability to maximize power, however, is not constant across authoritarian regimes; rather, it is a function of the environments in which leaders rule. Where authoritarian leaders *can* consolidate control, they will.

What Strategies Do Authoritarian Leaders Use to Maintain Power?

Authoritarian leaders face an ever-present threat to their rule. Not only are elites constantly vying to secure the leadership post themselves, but also latent mass unrest always has the potential to steamroll into an uprising. It should therefore be unsurprising that leadership insecurity pervades authoritarian politics.

Leaders tend to prioritize mitigating the threat elites pose to their rule over that of the masses. This is primarily because the probability that elites will oust them is typically higher in any given moment than the probability the masses will.

Leaders use a variety of tactics to lessen the danger that elites will remove them from power, all of which are complicated by the fact that they never truly know whether elites are their allies or rivals.[9] Elites have an incentive to conceal their true ambitions. Public displays of loyalty to the leader can mask behind-the-doors schemes to oust him. This generates a complex guessing game for the leader in terms of who he can and cannot trust.

As a result, authoritarian leaders expend substantial effort trying to lesson both: (1) the chance that elites will defect from the leadership group, and (2) their ability to join forces to do so. Because coups are the most common means through which authoritarian leaders leave power (discussed later on in this chapter), they also engage in coup-proofing.

To minimize the risk of elite defections, many leadership survival strategies involve rewarding and punishing members of the elite. Leaders will try to compensate their elite supporters as a means of incentivizing them to remain loyal, usually by assigning them choice political posts and/or giving them access to the perks of office. In North Korea in 2010, for example, then-leader Kim Jong Il promoted State Security Chief U Dong Chuk to the position of general in the Korean People's Army as a reward for serving as a "succession tutor" for his son, Kim Jong Un.[10] At the same time, leaders are quick to discipline those elites whose loyalty they question, both as a means of sidelining the individuals who could potentially oust them and to send a message to others in the inner circle that disloyalty is risky. Punishments can range in severity from job demotion to death. The experience of North Korea is illustrative here, too. In 2013, Kim Jong Un—who took over the leadership post after his father's death in 2011—executed his uncle and former mentor Jang Song Thaek for allegedly plotting a coup.[11]

In determining whether to continue supporting the leader, elites must calculate whether the benefits of doing so outweigh the costs and risks of defection. Changing circumstances can influence this assessment. An economic crisis, for example, may reduce the perks of backing the leader and incentivize elite defections. Other events, such as a corruption scandal that triggers mass protests, may also give elites reason to defect by signaling the leader's unpopularity and lessening the perceived risk of jumping ship. It should be noted that these calculations are not always obvious, and elites themselves may encounter difficulties accurately assessing them.

Of course, removing an authoritarian leader from power requires the backing of more than a single individual. Even coups, which can be executed with the support of just a handful of individuals, are not one-person efforts. An elite defector must join forces with other elite defectors to pose a real challenge to the dictator. For this reason, authoritarian leaders also try to factionalize the elite and keep them in competition with one another. This strategy is referred to as *divide and conquer*.[12] It entails frequently shuffling elites from one position to the next and hiring and firing them in ways that generate suspicion. The result is an environment of high uncertainty, such that elites are constantly unsure of their own standing vis-à-vis others within the leadership group. This prevents the formation of any particular group that could challenge the leader, while also keeping rivals from establishing their own independent power bases.[13]

As a final point, authoritarian leaders also engage in coup-proofing to protect their hold on power. Coups are a common method through which authoritarian leaders are overthrown, as mentioned earlier. They require the participation of at least some military officers, who are frequently themselves part of the leadership group or working on behalf of some of its members. To reduce the risk of a coup, authoritarian leaders pursue a number of tactics. These include interfering in military recruitment and promotions, with an eye toward stacking the military with loyalists to the leader; and creating parallel security forces to counterbalance the regular army, such as the establishment of a presidential guard to exclusively protect the leader.[14] In Iraq, for example, Saddam Hussein formed multiple armed groups to keep the threat of a military coup at bay, the most loyal of which was responsible for his personal protection.[15] It should be noted that though coup-proofing is designed to protect dictators from a military coup, in angering the military, it can actually set in motion the event it is intended to prevent.[16]

The ability of authoritarian leaders to pursue all these survival strategies varies from one context to the next, depending on a number of factors such as the balance of power between leaders and elites and the resources at the leader's disposal.

What Is Personalization?

Most authoritarian leaders try to secure personal control over as many major political instruments as they can while in office, such as assignments to political posts, policy directives, and the security forces. Some are successful in their efforts to maximize power, such as Alexander Lukashenko of Belarus, but others are not, such as Blaise Compaore of Burkina Faso, whose attempt to amend the constitution to extend his term in office in 2014 triggered a massive uprising that forced him to resign. We may not always be able to observe leader attempts to consolidate control, but we can generally assume that all authoritarian leaders are trying to do so.

Where dictators are successful in amassing greater political power into their own hands, they have moved the regime toward greater *personalization*. Personalization refers to the process through which leaders strengthen their own control over the regime. It signals a shift in the balance of power between the leader and elites in the leader's favor. This tilt in power relations typically endures until the leader leaves office, and in many instances intensifies over the course of the leader's tenure given that success in one power grab often begets success in others. Each grab for power means that the leader has accumulated even more of it, making it even more difficult for the elite to challenge such actions.[17] Personalization can occur in democracies as well, though free and fair electoral competition prevents it from ever reaching the levels that we see in authoritarian contexts.[18]

Personalization in authoritarian regimes usually occurs during the first few years after the regime seizes power, when it is still uncertain what the rules of the game will be.[19] About a third of all dictators successfully personalize the regimes they lead within this time frame.[20] Personalization can also occur later on in a regime's lifetime and ebb and flow over time. It can vary in terms of its scope as well, with leaders finding success in some but not all their efforts to personalize.

China under the Chinese Communist Party offers a good example of these dynamics. After the revolution in 1949, Mao carried out a number of actions to consolidate control, including executing scores of opponents to his rule.[21] By the time he died in 1976, power lay firmly in Mao's hands. After his death, however, the level of personalization declined, and China moved toward a more collegial system of rule. It has since swung back in the other direction under the leadership of Xi Jinping, though China has not yet reached the level of personalization now that it had under Mao.[22]

The causes of personalization are less well understood. We know that authoritarian leadership groups are better equipped to resist personalization when they are unified and well organized, such as is the case when the leadership group draws from a professionalized military or cohesive political party.[23] Such features make it easier for the inner circle to credibly commit to overthrow the leader for opportunistic behaviors, thereby preventing the leader from expanding the power of the executive.[24] We know less, however, about the conditions that give rise to authoritarian regimes that have leadership groups sharing these features in the first place.

What Are the Signs of Personalization?

There are a number of telltale indicators of personalization. This section will discuss six of the most common.[25] All these indicators reflect greater consolidation of power in the hands of the leader.

The first sign of personalization is narrowing of the inner circle. Some narrowing occurs in most authoritarian regimes after the seizure of power, but substantial narrowing is a sign that leaders have concentrated power.[26] By reducing the size of the support group, narrowing reduces the number of individuals with whom leaders must share policy influence and the spoils of office. In this way, it gives leaders greater control. In Russia, for example, observers estimate that only

20 to 30 individuals comprise Vladimir Putin's inner circle, all of whom are strong Putin allies with ties to the military and security sector. This group of individuals is said to make most decisions in Russia, and from within it come the half a dozen or so most powerful individuals in the country.[27]

The second sign of personalization is the installation of loyalists in key positions of power. Leaders seek to stack major government institutions—primarily the courts, the security sector, the military, and the civil service—with individuals who are their steadfast allies. In evaluating whom to promote, they prioritize loyalty over competence; trustworthiness trumps all else. As an example, Hugo Chavez of Venezuela installed Chavistas in major positions across a number of sectors, including the judiciary, central bank, and state-owned oil industry. When making such decisions, "technical ability [was] a secondary consideration to fealty."[28] At the same time, leaders try to purge key government institutions of those who oppose them, or at least neutralize their influence. In Turkey, for example, Recep Erdogan leveraged a failed coup in 2016 to initiate a purge of his opponents in the regime, including officials in the civil service, the judiciary, and the military.[29]

The third sign of personalization is the promotion of family members to powerful posts. Family members, like loyalists, are usually more trustworthy allies for authoritarian leaders than experts are. Leaders therefore try to put them in positions of influence, even if they lack government experience (which is often the case). By surrounding themselves with family members, leaders ensure that they have individuals whom they can rely on to implement their vision of governance. Iraq under Saddam Hussein exemplifies this tactic well. Hussein promoted members of his family to major positions in the security forces, even though all of them lacked the appropriate qualifications. His son Qusay led the Revolutionary Guard, his son Uday controlled the Fedayeens, and his cousin Barzan Abd al-Ghafur ran the Special Republican Guard.[30]

The fourth sign of personalization is the creation of a new political party or movement. Leaders seek to establish new political organizations or movements as a means of lessening the influence of the traditional political establishment and marginalizing rivals who could challenge them. Doing so also provides leaders with a new vehicle they can use to organize their supporters. One example of this is Alberto Fujimori's creation of Cambio 90 in Peru, which he established in 1990 and used to back his subsequent power grab in 1992. Another example of this is Chavez's establishment of the Fifth Republic Movement in Venezuela in 1997, which a decade later became the United Socialist Party of Venezuela, the major party Chavez relied on for support.

The fifth sign of personalization is the use of referendums or plebiscites as a means of making key decisions. Leaders typically use this tactic as a way of cementing constitutional changes and other moves that bestow greater powers on them. By appealing directly to the public, these votes give such decisions greater legitimacy, even though they are rarely true reflections of the people's will. A classic example may be derived from Nazi Germany. The German government held a referendum in 1934, which it used to get public approval for the decision to merge the authority of the president of the Reich with the office of the chancellor. The vast majority of voters voted "yes," and Hitler's powers were enhanced afterward.[31]

Finally, the sixth sign of personalization is the creation of new security services. The goal of this move is to counterbalance the traditional military in hopes of deterring officers from staging a coup (i.e., coup-proofing). Though this tactic is risky (because the military may actually stage a coup in protest should they catch wind of the dictator's intentions), once leaders have succeeded in creating a new armed organization, it is a signal that they have substantially consolidated control. The existence of a loyal security force that lies outside of the realm of the traditional military lessens the likelihood of military ouster and, as a consequence, the bargaining power of the military vis-à-vis the leader. As an example, Francois Duvalier of Haiti created the Tonton Macoutes in 1959, which was a group of fiercely loyal young men armed with machetes organized to protect him.[32] The group acted as a security police force and before long eclipsed the military in its powers.

What Are the Consequences of Personalization for Political Outcomes in Authoritarian Regimes?

Personalization of power means that power is consolidated in the hands of the leader. Political systems with such features are referred to as personalist dictatorships (described in more detail in Chapter 5). In personalist dictatorships, leaders govern absent constraints on their rule and can pursue the policies of their choosing. It is difficult for elites to hold them accountable for their actions, and—as a result—leaders can make bad choices without facing repercussions for doing so. Leaders in personalist dictatorships typically surround themselves with loyal as opposed to competent advisors. Anyone deemed disloyal is usually purged, turning elites into a group of sycophants.

Research shows that these dynamics lead to negative consequences across a range of political outcomes.[33] For one, personalist dictatorships are the most prone to corruption of all authoritarian regimes.[34] Leaders distribute resources to a narrow group of supporters on the basis of clientelism, enabling corruption to easily flourish. Institutional checks on the leader's actions are weak, facilitating abuses of power.

Personalist dictatorships are also the most likely form of authoritarianism to initiate interstate conflicts.[35] They can engage in risky activities without fearing domestic punishment for having done so. They are the most likely to invest in nuclear weapons as well.[36] Leaders in personalist dictatorships more frequently see nuclear weapons as an appealing solution to their security concerns, and they are able to pursue such programs without constraints. Personalist dictatorships are the most likely type of dictatorship to make foreign policy mistakes, too.[37] They typically surround themselves with individuals who simply tell them what they want to hear out of fear of reprisal, preventing them from receiving accurate information about foreign policy issues from their subordinates.

The list of negative consequences goes on. Among authoritarian regimes, personalist dictatorships are the least likely to engage in cooperative behavior. [38] They can refuse to sign international agreements because their leaders have more flexibility to act as they choose. Personalist dictatorships are the form of dictatorship most likely to squander foreign aid as well.[39] They can use aid to pad their pocketbooks and those of their supporters as a means of prolonging their rule. The experience of the Democratic Republic of Congo (then Zaire) under Mobutu Sese Seku is a classic example of this behavior.

And, perhaps most troubling, personalist dictatorships are the least likely of all authoritarian regimes to democratize upon their collapse.[40] Their leaders hold on to power until the bitter end in the face of challenges to their rule and, as such, their transitions are often protracted and bloody. The ousters of Saddam Hussein in Iraq and Muammar Gaddafi in Libya illustrate this well. The hollowed-out institutions that personalist dictatorships leave behind result in an environment that bodes poorly for democratization. As a result, personalist dictatorships frequently transition after their collapse to a new dictatorship (e.g., Cambodia after Pol Pot) or failed state (e.g., Somalia after Siad Barre).

To summarize, concentration of power generates political dynamics that set in motion a host of negative political outcomes for global peace and prosperity. Among authoritarian regimes, those in which a single leader has consolidated control—that is, personalist dictatorships—are associated with a broad range of bad behaviors, ranging from starting wars to misusing aid.

This suggests that those in the international community would be wise to pay close attention to the behaviors of authoritarian leaders and assess whether they exemplify any of the telltale signs of personalization. Though personalization is often difficult to reverse while the leaders who succeeded in doing it are still in office, a first step to pushing back against such developments is being able to quickly identify when they are taking place to begin with.

How Do Authoritarian Leaders Leave Power?

Unlike in democracies, leaders in authoritarian regimes can rarely be voted out of office. Most end up departing in far less enjoyable ways. The methods through which authoritarian leaders usually leave power fall into two broad categories: insider-led exits and outsider-led exits.[41] In addition, some authoritarian leaders die in office.

There are two key types of insider-led exits: coups and "regular" removals from office. Coups are forced ousters the military carries out, typically senior officers who are themselves part of the regime elite or junior officers who are tied to the regime by virtue of their military affiliation. An example of the former is the 1991 overthrow of President Moussa Traore in Mali at the hands of his presidential guard; an example of the latter is the 1967 junior officer–led coup that toppled General Christophe Soglo in Benin. "Regular" removals from office are insider-led exits that do not entail the use of force.[42] These include conditions such as enforced term limits, resignations, consensus decisions on behalf of a politburo or military junta, and (rarely) elections that leaders lose. It is reasonable to assume that such exits are due to the pressures of regime insiders, given that authoritarian leaders' primary goal is to maintain power and we would not expect them to voluntarily choose to relinquish it. "Regular" removals imply a regime elite powerful enough to compel leaders to leave office without having to resort to force. Examples include the departures of a string of Mexican presidents during the decades-long rule of the Institutional Revolutionary Party (PRI). The party was so organizationally strong that it was able to implement the *dedazo* tradition, in which its leaders chose their successor and then stepped down after six years in power. Other examples include the resignations of Boris Yeltsin in Russia in 1999, which some have suggested Kremlin strategists timed to ensure that their preferred successor, Vladimir Putin, would secure the presidency,[43] and of Levon Ter-Petrosyan in Armenia in 1998, which came after tensions between Ter-Petrosyan and a number of key government ministers escalated over how to handle the Nagorno–Karabakh conflict with Armenia.

There are two main types of mass-led exits: insurgencies and popular uprisings. These modes of overthrow are fairly self-explanatory. In both instances, some mass group (a rebel organization in the case of an insurgency and ordinary citizens in the case of a popular uprising) forces the leader out of power, regardless of the level of violence involved. Samuel Doe's overthrow at the hands of rebels in 1990 in Liberia exemplifies ouster via insurgency, while Hosni Mubarak's overthrow following a series of mass demonstrations in 2011 in Egypt exemplifies ouster via popular uprising.

Finally, some dictators die in office, either due to assassination (e.g., Rafael Trujillo of the Dominican Republic in 1961) or natural causes (e.g., Kim Jong Il of North Korea in 2011).

From 1950 to 2012, there were 473 authoritarian leaders who left power. Regime insiders were responsible for the majority (65 percent) of these exits, with coups and "regular" removals from office each accounting for about a third of all leader exits. Twenty percent of authoritarian leaders died in office, and only 10 percent were kicked out at the hands of the masses (3 percent via insurgency and 7 percent via popular uprising). The remaining 5 percent of authoritarian leader overthrows occurred either via foreign invasion (e.g., Manuel Noriega of Panama, who was toppled by U.S. forces in 1989) or some other method that is difficult to classify.

These numbers illustrate why authoritarian leaders so frequently fear regime elites: insider-led exits vastly outnumber all other modes of leaving power. In addition, though most of the time the use of force is required to get authoritarian leaders to leave office, about a third of the time it is not, with leaders leaving instead via "regular" means. The violent ouster of a dictator may be the image we have in mind when thinking about an authoritarian leader exiting power, but on occasion elite actors are sufficiently powerful as a collective to compel leaders to do so without having to actually put a gun to their heads. Lastly, death in office is perhaps more common than we might assume. About one in five dictators dies while in power. This is likely a reflection of the extent to which authoritarian leaders value staying in office over all else; they will rule until their last breaths, if they can get away with doing so.

How Are Authoritarian Leaders Most Likely to Leave Power Today?

There have been a number of important changes over the course of the post–World War II period in terms of how authoritarian leaders leave power. Figure 4.1, which offers the breakdown of authoritarian leader exits by decade, illustrates this.

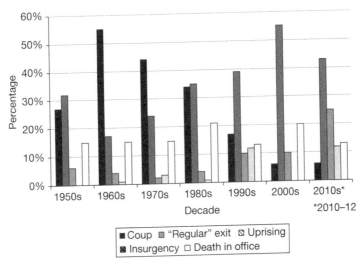

Figure 4.1 How dictators fall: 1950 to 2012.

First, it shows that though insider-led departures (coups and "regular" exits) are still the most common way in which authoritarian leaders depart office, they have declined considerably in recent years. In the 1960s, for example, insider-led exits comprised more than 70 percent of all leader exits, a number that decreased to under 50 percent in the period from 2010 to 2012. This reduction in the frequency of insider-led exits is due to the substantial drop in coups; "regular" removals from office actually increased during the period.

The data show that coups have diminished dramatically as a form of authoritarian leader ouster since the end of the Cold War. Whereas coups made up more than half (55 percent) of all authoritarian leader exits at their peak in the 1960s, this number has fallen to only around 6 percent since 2000. This is consistent with research suggesting that changes in the geopolitical priorities of the West after the Cold War's end led to a decline in military dictatorships and consequently a decline in coups, given that coups are the key method of leadership turnover in such regimes.[44] The end of the Cold War also led to legislation in the United States and the European Union that pledged withdrawal of foreign aid should a recipient country experience a coup, disincentivizing plotters from staging coups and lowering their frequency.[45]

At the same time, "regular" removals of authoritarian leaders from office have actually increased over time, going from less than a quarter of all leader exits in the 1960s and 1970s to 44 percent from 2010 to 2012. This increase primarily reflects the prominence of authoritarian regimes with strong political parties in recent years, some of which feature elites with influence over leadership selection and removal, such as the Communist regimes in China and Vietnam.[46]

Mass-led exits (popular uprisings and insurgencies) are also on the rise since the end of the Cold War. Such departures made up around 5 percent of all authoritarian leader exits throughout the Cold War, a number that more than doubled after it. Insurgencies, for example, accounted for only a handful of leader exits during the Cold War, but became more common afterward—particularly in the 1990s—in line with the global rise in civil wars that occurred at the time of the collapse of the Soviet Union.[47] They made up a little more than 10 percent of all authoritarian exits in the period from 2010 to 2012. Popular uprisings also appear to be on the rise. During the Cold War, they made up less than 5 percent of all authoritarian leader exits. In the 2010 to 2012 period, however, this number skyrocketed to 25 percent. Examples include the overthrow of Kurmanbek Bakiyev in Kyrgyzstan in 2010 and Zine el-Abidine Ben Ali in Tunisia in 2011. There are a number of potential reasons for this rise, such as the fact that many authoritarian regimes since the end of the Cold War tolerate greater political competition, which likely improves citizens' ability to hit the streets and mobilize.[48]

It is perhaps too soon to know whether this dramatic rise in popular uprisings will persist in the years to come. The data suggest, however, that mass uprisings are becoming a growing challenge to authoritarian leaders. Should this trend continue, we will likely see a change in the strategies that authoritarian leaders use to maintain power, such that addressing mass preferences will become a greater priority.

What Happens to Authoritarian Leaders Once They Leave Power?

For some authoritarian leaders, leaving power leads to a peaceful life of retirement. For others, however, it brings with it a far worse fate.

The data indicate that a majority of leaders have fared well after leaving office: 59 percent of all authoritarian leaders simply went on to live their normal lives after their departures from power.[49] Examples include Mikhail Gorbachev, who left power in 1991 upon the collapse of the Soviet Union and remains active in Russian politics to this day, and Nikita Khrushchev, who ruled the Soviet Union until 1964 when the Soviet elite removed him and he went on to receive a regime-sponsored monthly pension and housing.[50]

On the flip side, this statistic means that 41 percent of authoritarian leaders have not fared well after leaving office. Twenty percent of authoritarian leaders fell from power and were forced into exile (e.g., Alberto Fujimori of Peru in 2000), 12 percent were imprisoned (e.g., Manuel Noriega of Panama in 1989), and 9 percent were killed (e.g., Nicolae Ceausescu of Romania in 1989). These numbers are high enough that they likely factor into the decisions of authoritarian leaders while in power.

How Does Fear of Punishment after Leaving Power Affect the Behavior of Leaders While in Office?

A leader's prospects tomorrow strongly condition the actions of today. This is true of all leaders, whether dictators or democrats. Authoritarian leaders, however, face a higher chance of post-tenure punishment than do their democratic counterparts. This is largely because democratic leaders are far more likely to leave power via free and fair elections, virtually guaranteeing them a safe exit. Authoritarian regimes, by contrast, typically lack established mechanisms for transferring power from one leader to the next, and smooth leadership turnovers are less common. Leadership transitions in authoritarian regimes are far more likely to occur via force, in turn increasing the chance that leaders will face a "bad" fate.[51] Though more authoritarian leaders fare well after leaving power than fare poorly, more than a third can still expect to be sent into exile, imprisoned, or killed upon leaving office, as mentioned earlier.

This is important because research indicates that when leaders worry that they will face punishment after leaving office, they become more willing to engage in risky behavior.[52] The prospect of encountering a bad fate post-tenure strongly increases the chance of aggression toward other states. Conflict is a risky decision for leaders: while a win could boost domestic popularity, a loss could also spell their ouster. This type of a gamble is usually not in the interest of leaders whose tenures are secure and whose chances of punishment after leaving office are minimal. For those who are politically vulnerable and at risk of a bad fate should they lose power, however, it can be an attractive strategy. As such, when leaders are likely to face punishment when unseated from power, they are more likely to resort to conflict to avert their potential overthrow.

The empirical evidence supports this: as the threat of post-tenure punishment increases, so does the likelihood that leaders will initiate conflicts.[53] This helps to explain why authoritarian leaders are more belligerent than democratic ones.[54]

The experience of Uganda under Idi Amin is illustrative of this. Amin, who assumed power in 1971, was increasingly unpopular as his tenure progressed. His disastrous economic policies and extreme use of brutality against both ordinary citizens and the elite made him hated by many. In 1978, a mysterious car accident killed his vice president, General Mustafa Adrisi, prompting a rebellion among troops loyal to him. Amin, with good reason, feared he would be overthrown. Soon thereafter, in an effort to divert attention from his domestic woes, Amin invaded Tanzania and annexed part of its territory.[55]

In addition to conflict initiation, there is evidence that authoritarian leaders who fear a costly removal from office are more likely to repress their citizens.[56] When leaders perceive that threats to their rule are high, they are more likely to use repression in an attempt to thwart their overthrow.

Not surprisingly, leaders who are likely to encounter bad fates are more likely to cling to power until the very end. As a consequence, when they do leave power, their departures are often violent, they frequently trigger the collapse of the regime, and the new regime that emerges afterward is typically authoritarian in form.[57]

When Authoritarian Leaders Leave Power, What Is Likely to Happen to the Regime?

Authoritarian regimes collapse with authoritarian leaders about half of the time.[58] This means that we should be careful about distinguishing authoritarian leaders from the regimes they lead when analyzing authoritarian politics, as discussed in Chapter 2. The leader's departure by no means guarantees that the regime will go down as well.

That said, how an authoritarian leader falls from power can tell us quite a bit about whether regime collapse is likely to accompany it. For example, the data indicate that regime change is most apt to occur concurrently with leadership change when leaders exit through force. Leaders overthrown via insurgency or popular uprising, for example, see their regimes ousted along with them quite frequently (87 percent and 85 percent of the time, respectively). This is to be expected given that both forms of ouster are typically part of broader efforts for political change.

Perhaps surprisingly, coups only lead to regime change about half of the time (52 percent). Though coups entail the use of force, the collapse of the regime is often not the plotters' goal. In military dictatorships, for example, coups are simply the way that elites "vote" leaders out of power, akin to no-confidence votes in parliamentary systems.[59] For this reason, the regime remains intact even after the leader is overthrown.

"Regular" removals from office propel the downfall of the regime in 42 percent of cases. Often these transfers of power are part of institutionalized succession processes, designed explicitly for the purpose of protecting the regime from the vulnerability that can accompany leadership succession. The experience of Mexico under the PRI during most of the twentieth century exemplifies this, as does that of China under the Chinese Communist Party post-Mao. Less frequently, "regular" removals from office are the result of negotiations between the regime leadership and other actors for the regime to leave power. In such instances, regime collapse accompanies that of the leader intentionally, as part of a bargaining arrangement. This was the case in Argentina in 1983, when General Reynaldo Bignone and the ruling military elite negotiated the military's retreat from power following its disastrous performance in the Falklands War.

Importantly, though observers often speculate that a dictator's death will incite destabilizing political infighting that will bring about a regime's collapse, this is rarely the case.[60] Death in office—regardless of whether it occurs via assassination or natural causes—infrequently leads to regime change. This is largely due to the fact that dictators who die in office tend to be particularly adept at governing; the fact that they remained in power until the very end suggests that regime elites opted to remain loyal to them up until that juncture. Such leaders therefore usually leave behind them a set of regime actors highly motivated to preserve the status quo. Indeed, in only 9 percent of cases do regimes fall from power when their leaders die in office. Instead, regime continuity is the norm, as was true following the deaths of Hugo Chavez in Venezuela in 2012 and Kim Jong Il in North Korea the year prior.

To summarize, when authoritarian leaders leave power, their regimes do not always do the same. The mode of leadership transition, however, is telling. Regime collapse is very common when leaders are pushed out of office via broad-based efforts, such as insurgencies or popular uprisings. It is far less likely when leaders exit peacefully, as is often the case with "regular" removals from office. And it is highly unlikely when leaders die.

5

AUTHORITARIAN REGIME TYPES

How Do Authoritarian Regimes Differ from One Another?

Authoritarian regimes sometimes can seem more different from one another than they are from democracies. As an extreme example, take two authoritarian regimes that have governed in southern Africa for the bulk of the last few decades (both in power at the time of writing): one in Zimbabwe and one in Botswana. The Zimbabwe African National Union–Patriotic Front (ZANU–PF) is currently in charge of the former, and the Botswana Democratic Party (BDP) is currently in charge of the latter. Yet, how politics worked in each of these regimes has been dramatically different. In Zimbabwe, Robert Mugabe was the regime's only leader from 1980 to 2017, and—even though he was 93 at the time of his overthrow—he showed little intention of ever stepping down prior. His wife, Grace Mugabe, stated in 2017, for example, that he should run "as a corpse" in the 2018 elections if he died before the vote.[1] Power was concentrated in Mugabe's hands, human rights abuses were widespread, and Zimbabwe's corruption ranking was 154th (out of 176 countries), making it one of the most corrupt countries in the world.[2] It is doubtful that much will change under his successor, Emmerson Mnangagwa. In Botswana, by contrast, Ian Khama is the regime's fourth leader and, due to term limits, likely to step down once his term expires.[3]

Substantial political power lies with the BDP, which can provide a check on the leadership. Botswana is the least corrupt country in Africa and one of the least corrupt countries in the world (with a ranking of 35).[4] Moreover, though Botswana is considered authoritarian in this book because of evidence of unequal playing fields in its elections,[5] a number of observers actually classify it as democratic.[6] In other words, Botswana appears to have more in common with a democracy such as the one in Ghana than it does with an authoritarian regime such as the one that governs Zimbabwe.

As this comparison illustrates, authoritarian regimes can differ from one another in important ways and along a variety of fronts, including the institutions they rely on to maintain power, the extent to which they allow electoral competition, the constraints leaders face on their rule, how much they repress their populations, and how much they steal from the state, to name a few.

What Are the Different Types of Political Institutions Featured in Authoritarian Regimes?

Authoritarian regimes lack the truly free and fair elections that are the defining feature of democracies, but otherwise the political institutions they incorporate are quite similar in form. Many authoritarian regimes rely on a political party for support, and some also allow opposition parties to participate in the political process. Legislatures are widespread in authoritarian regimes as well, and though regime supporters dominate most authoritarian legislatures, in some the opposition has substantial representation. Elections are also common in authoritarian regimes, and they are often held on a regular basis. Elections are extremely heterogeneous across authoritarian regimes, with their only shared trait being the absence of true competitiveness. Some authoritarian elections fall just short of free and fair contests for one reason or another, while others are predetermined charades with only a single candidate on the ballot. Regardless of the nature of the electoral contest, authoritarian regimes go to great lengths to ensure that they emerge victorious.

In sum, political institutions in authoritarian regimes are generally similar in form to those we see in democracies. Though some authoritarian regimes feature none of these pseudo-democratic political institutions, most incorporate at least one of them, and many include all of them.

How and Why Are the Authoritarian Regimes of Today Different from Those of the Past?

Today's authoritarian regimes differ from their Cold War–era predecessors primarily in terms of the extent to which they seek to mimic democratic rule. For example, democratic-looking political institutions are common in authoritarian regimes, but even more so since the end of the Cold War. During the Cold War, 89 percent of all authoritarian regimes governed with a support party at some point while they were in power, 80 percent allowed more than one political party to operate, 73 percent featured a legislature, and 66 held at least one election.[7] All these statistics increased after the Cold War. Since 1990, 94 percent of all authoritarian regimes have governed with a support party at some point while in power, 87 percent allowed more than one political party to operate, 87 percent featured a legislature, and 71 percent have held at least one election. These statistics illustrate that not only do most authoritarian regimes incorporate political institutions that appear similar to those of democracies, but they are also increasingly likely to do so since the Cold War's end.

Beyond their reliance on pseudo-democratic political institutions, today's authoritarian regimes are increasingly imitating democracies in other ways as well.[8] Examples include letting nongovernmental organizations operate but secretly requiring them to promote the government line, deploying election monitors but covertly paying them to ensure they validate the contest's results, and hiring public relations firms to promote a favorable image of the regime at home and abroad.

All these moves reflect an effort on the part of today's authoritarian regimes to feign democratic rule as a means of making it more difficult to allege that they are authoritarian. Imitating democratic governance has a variety of benefits for today's authoritarian regimes, ranging from making it easier for them to attract foreign aid to helping them deflect any criticism of their rule.

Their Cold War predecessors had few reasons to promote such illusions. The pseudo-democratic institutions they featured helped them prolong their rule (for reasons discussed in Chapter 7), but they were not necessarily required to stay in the good graces of the international community. Since the end of the Cold War, however, democracy has emerged as the preferred form of government, both in the eyes of key international actors and among many domestic audiences.[9] Authoritarian regimes therefore have incentives to disguise their true authoritarian nature behind the façade of democracy.

For these reasons, the key way in which today's authoritarian regimes differ from those of decades past is in terms of the extent to which they seek to mimic democracies.

Why Is It Important to Differentiate Authoritarian Regimes from One Another?

Authoritarian regimes vary from one another in a number of ways, and differences across them are systematically tied to differences in their behavior. Disaggregating dictatorships, therefore, can reveal important distinctions in terms of how politics works in authoritarian contexts and, consequently, the types of political outcomes we are likely to see. These outcomes include the extent to which authoritarian regimes rely on repression, their propensity for civil war, their vulnerabilities to economic sanctions, the risk they will collapse at any given moment, and their chances of democratization, to name a few.[10]

For this reason, scholars have proposed a number of ways of differentiating authoritarian regimes. These typologies represent efforts to break down the category "authoritarian" into subcategories that shed light on differences in their behaviors. Most typologies fall under one of two categories: continuous and categorical.[11] Because they usually emphasize concepts that scholars can measure cross-nationally, typologies of authoritarianism have enabled empirical evaluations of the impact of authoritarian regime "type" on a range of political outcomes of importance.

What Are Continuous Typologies?

Continuous typologies differentiate authoritarian regimes according to how "authoritarian" they are. Using this approach, authoritarianism is a concept that can be placed on a continuum, and there are different gradients of authoritarian rule. Continuous typologies typically position authoritarian regimes on a democratic-autocratic scale, with fully democratic systems put on one end, fully authoritarian systems on the other, and systems that are mixtures of both somewhere in between.

Continuous typologies therefore bring to the surface the fact that many authoritarian regimes integrate features of democratic governance in their system of rule. In such regimes, we might see the leadership hold elections that the opposition can run in but from a disadvantaged position, an electoral playing field that is competitive but never truly fair, the media disproportionately favoring the incumbent, and electoral rules tailored to ensure incumbent victories. Scholars have used a number of labels to refer to these types of authoritarian regimes that fall in the middle of the democratic-autocratic spectrum—including "hybrid," "gray-zone,"[12] "competitive authoritarian,"[13] and "electoral authoritarian."[14] Regardless of the label used, a central assumption is that these regimes are "less" authoritarian than are dictatorships with more restrictive political environments.

There are a number of data sets that use continuous typologies to capture "levels" of authoritarianism, including the widely used Polity data set[15] and Freedom House's measures of political rights and civil liberties.[16] Using such data sets, we can capture a number of interesting developments across countries, such as the slow deterioration of Venezuelan democracy that began in 1992 with the failed coup led by Hugo Chavez and has continued since. Venezuela remained democratic until 2005, after which it transitioned to authoritarianism. With these data sources, we can also measure the steady decline in Hungarian democracy that has occurred since Viktor Orban and the Fidesz coalition came to power in 2010, as well as the democratic gains achieved in Myanmar since 2010 after the military's formal transition out of power. Most continue to see Hungary as democratic and Myanmar as authoritarian, but both have clearly moved in opposing directions on the democratic-autocratic spectrum.

What Are "Hybrid" Regimes?

In a number of countries, the regime in power is neither fully democratic nor fully authoritarian, as discussed in the directly preceding section. These regimes are frequently referred to as "hybrid" regimes. "Hybrid" regimes fall in the "gray zone" of the democratic-autocratic spectrum, combining both democratic and autocratic traits.[17] Theoretically, "hybrid" regimes are rooted in the continuous typology perspective, which views authoritarianism as something that can be placed on a continuum.

"Electoral authoritarian" and "competitive authoritarian" are terms that refer to hybrid regimes that lie more toward the autocratic side of the spectrum, while "flawed democratic" and "defective democratic" are terms that refer to hybrid regimes that lie more toward the democratic side of the spectrum. Typically, whether a hybrid regime leans more democratic than autocratic "turns crucially on the freedom, fairness, inclusiveness, and meaningfulness of elections."[18]

What Are Categorical Typologies?

Categorical typologies disaggregate authoritarian regimes according to specific features of their rule. Using this approach, "levels" of authoritarianism are constant across authoritarian regimes; their differences are instead based on other dimensions, such as the strategies leaders use to maintain power and the groups from which leaders and elites originate.

Categorical typologies illuminate the heterogeneity of authoritarian regimes, not in terms of the extent to which they seek to imitate democracies, but in a variety of other domains. A handful emphasize differences across authoritarian regimes in the strategies leaders pursue to maintain power[19]; most, however, look at differences in their makeup, such as whether leaders come from the military or a civilian organization.

There are a number of data sets that classify authoritarian regimes using categorical typologies, including those of Barbara Geddes, Joseph Wright, and Erica Frantz (which groups them based on whether they are dominant-party, military, monarchic, or personalist); Michael Wahman, Jan Teorell, and Axel Hadenius (which groups them based on whether they are multiparty, one-party, military, monarchic, or no-party); and Jose Antonio Cheibub, Jennifer Gandhi, and James Raymond Vreeland (which groups them based on whether their leaders are military officers, civilians, or monarchs).[20]

Which Typology Is "Best"?

The development of typologies to differentiate authoritarian regimes has made it easier for scholars to compare dictatorships and better understand the consequences of differences in how they rule.[21] This represents a significant advance in the field of authoritarian politics because authoritarian regimes are no longer seen as monolithic. That said, there is no single typology that is universally superior to the others. Both continuous and categorical approaches have their advantages and drawbacks, as do the specific typologies that they encompass.

Continuous typologies, for example, allow us to rate some authoritarian regimes as "less" authoritarian than others. This is beneficial because it is likely that these mid-range authoritarian regimes differ from their fully authoritarian counterparts in important ways, most notably in terms of the political rights their citizens enjoy. At the same time, continuous typologies assume that as regimes move away from the authoritarian end of the political spectrum, they are closer to being democracies. This is not necessarily true (a point emphasized in Chapter 8). "Levels" of authoritarianism are not always good predictors of likely transitions to democracy.

Categorical typologies, by contrast, view all authoritarian regimes as equally authoritarian, enabling us to avoid making the questionable assumption that authoritarianism is a linear concept. By differentiating authoritarian regimes according to specific features of their rule, they can shed light on which features matter most for understanding key outcomes of interest, such as regime survival and democratization. Moreover, as an increasing number of authoritarian regimes today incorporate some features of democracy, as discussed earlier, differentiating regimes based on whether they do may begin to lose relevance. The disadvantage of categorical typologies, of course, is that they miss movements away from or toward democracy that we might care about, such as an authoritarian regime undergoing a lengthy process of political liberalization.

There have been extensive debates in the field of authoritarian politics regarding which typology is most representative of the nuances of authoritarian rule.[22] One of the major messages that emerges from these conversations is that the "best" typology depends on the specific question of interest.

Observers should take great care, however, to ensure that the theoretical concepts that they emphasize match the specific typology they use to capture them.

What Is the Regime Typology Emphasized in This Chapter and Why?

Much of this book discusses the ways in which the interactions of authoritarian actors influence how politics works. To inform the discussion, this chapter disaggregates authoritarian regimes according to their institutional structures, given that such structures shape the nature of these interactions. The specific typology this book relies on therefore differentiates authoritarian regimes based on the type of institution that constrains the leadership, whether it is a military (military dictatorship), single political party (dominant-party dictatorship), ruling family (monarchic dictatorship), or none of these (personalist dictatorship).[23] (Note that these are general categories; occasionally, regimes mix features of multiple types, such as Iran under the theocracy that has governed since 1979.) This typology is not necessarily appropriate for many questions scholars seek to answer in the field of authoritarian politics, but it is appropriate for those discussed in this chapter. These particular types of authoritarian regimes will be referenced in subsequent chapters as well, where relevant.

Note that because there have been so few monarchic dictatorships historically—there are only seven in power at the time of writing—it is difficult to make meaningful inferences about their behavior. The discussion will therefore focus on the other three types of authoritarian regimes.

What Is Military Dictatorship?

Military dictatorship is authoritarian rule in which the military as an institution is in control.[24] Military officers hold power, select who will fill the leadership post, and make policy choices. These individuals collectively are often referred to as a junta; most are senior (as opposed to junior) officers. In military dictatorships, elites mostly come from the military, as does the de facto leader. Occasionally, such regimes place "puppets" in the leadership position to pay lip service to civilian rule even though these individuals, in fact, have little power. Panama from 1982 to 1989 is an example of this: General Manuel Noriega was the de facto leader of the regime, but a string of civilians officially served as the president.

The structure of military dictatorships usually reflects that of the military itself, such that the military's form is essentially transferred to the political sphere. Military dictatorships typically feature a clear, hierarchical organization of authority; some even have rules in place for rotating power.[25] Critically, military elites are powerful enough in military dictatorships to constrain the actions of the leader.

Since World War II, military dictatorships have been particularly prevalent in Latin America, with the majority of the region's countries having at some point experienced this form of authoritarian rule. As one scholar wrote in 1999, "In no part of the developing world has the influence of the military been more profound than in Latin America. Political intervention and rule by the military have been almost the norm and not the regrettable exception."[26] Part of the reason for this lies in Cold War geopolitics. Because of the region's close proximity to the United States, the United States devoted substantial aid to Latin American militaries to ensure they were anti-Communist and, in some cases, directly assisted them in executing coups against democratically elected leaders, as occurred in Chile in 1973. Military dictatorships have also been common in sub-Saharan Africa, though to a lesser degree than in Latin America.

Examples of military dictatorship include Brazil (1964–1985), Ghana (1972–1979), and Turkey (1980–1983).

When a Leader Wears a Military Uniform, Does That Signal Military Dictatorship?

Many authoritarian leaders wear military uniforms. This tells us little, however, about whether the regime is a military dictatorship, as conceptualized here.[27] The definition of military dictatorship referenced earlier emphasizes the military as an institution in government, not simply a single military officer. It implies as well that other members of the military can influence the leader's choices.

As examples, though Idi Amin of Uganda and Muammar Gaddafi of Libya both wore military uniforms, neither of their regimes was a military dictatorship. Under both rulers, power was concentrated in their hands and few other actors could challenge them, classic characteristics of personalist rule. By contrast, in the Brazilian military dictatorship, generals served a single presidential term, and in the latest Argentine military dictatorship (from 1976 to 1983), the junta implemented a rotating presidency among its members. Military officials held key positions of power in both regimes and the military elite was powerful enough to constrain the leadership.

While it is safe to assume that military dictatorship implies a man in uniform in the leadership post, the converse is not true. Some leaders who are current or former military officers govern military dictatorships, but many others do not.

What Is Dominant-Party Dictatorship?

Dominant-party dictatorship is an authoritarian regime in which a single political party controls leadership selection and policy.[28] Members of the party hold the majority of key political posts, and regime elites typically come from the party's ruling body, often referred to as a politburo or central committee. The leader is usually the leader of the party as well. Though a single party controls the levers of power, other parties may legally exist in dominant-party dictatorships, and they may be allowed to contest elections and occasionally win them. Even when other parties hold a number of legislative seats, however, true political power lies with the dominant party. A relevant example is Singapore, where the 2015 legislative election gave 83 out of 89 seats to the People's Action Party, but 6 to the Worker's Party (an opposition party). The opposition has representation in the legislature, though power is tilted toward the ruling party.

With the exception of many of the Communist dominant-party dictatorships that governed during the Cold War, the structure of dominant-party dictatorships is often quite similar to the structure of democracies. Most are either presidential or parliamentary: if the regime uses a presidential system, then it mirrors a presidential democracy; the same is true if it is a parliamentary system. Importantly, party elites are powerful actors in dominant-party dictatorships and have the capacity to influence the actions of the leader.

Since World War II, dominant-party dictatorships have been particularly prevalent in Eastern Europe, parts of Africa, and Asia. Their distribution is explained by two factors. The first factor is Cold War geopolitics, with those countries falling under the Soviet Union's sphere of influence often adopting dominant-party systems of authoritarian rule. This is certainly the case for much of Eastern Europe, but also true of many dominant-party regimes in Asia. In the case of Africa, though the Soviet Union propped up a few of the dominant-party dictatorships there, more frequently they emerged on the heels of the independence movements that swept across the region in the decades that followed the end of World War II. In countries such as Namibia, Kenya, and Botswana, a political party led the independence effort and simply stayed in power afterward.

Examples of dominant-party dictatorship include Angola (1975–), Mexico (1915–2000), and Cote d'Ivoire (1960–1999).

Does the Existence of a Regime Support Party Signal Dominant-Party Dictatorship?

Most authoritarian regimes govern with the support of a political party. In fact, 91 percent of authoritarian regimes featured at least one political party in the post–World War II period at some point while in power. In more than half of these cases, however, the support party had little real political influence and, as such, these regimes are not dominant-party dictatorships. (Chapter 7 discusses the purposes of support parties.)

As an example, consider the fact that Saddam Hussein governed Iraq from 1979 to 2003, all the while in alliance with the Baath Party. Elites within the party could do little to guide Hussein's actions, instead serving to simply carry out his wishes. In a similar fashion, General Omar Torrijos and the military led Panama from 1968 to 1982. At first the regime banned political parties, but in 1978 it legalized them and created the Revolutionary Democratic Party (PRD) to organize its supporters. Yet, the PRD had little political weight and could not constrain Torrijos or help shape policy.

Because the vast majority of authoritarian regimes govern with the assistance of a support party, the existence of such parties should not be seen as an indicator of dominant-party rule. Categorizing a regime as such requires greater knowledge about the de facto power of the party's elite members. As a quick snapshot, however, the party elite are typically more powerful when the party organization predated the regime's assumption to power.[29]

What Is Personalist Dictatorship?

Personalist dictatorships fit the classic stereotype of authoritarian rule. In personalist dictatorships, power lies in the hands of the leader.[30] The leader controls access to key political posts, as well as most major policy decisions. The leader may wear a military uniform or govern with the support of a political party, but neither institution exercises power independently of the leader. In personalist dictatorships, elites typically are family members of the leader or loyal allies.

To be clear, in nearly all authoritarian regimes, leaders disproportionately wield political influence. In personalist dictatorships, however, this is extremely tilted, such that there are no political institutions that are autonomous. Leaders keep the elite on their toes, ensuring that no faction among them ever becomes too powerful. As one observer wrote regarding Mobutu Sese Seku in then Zaire, "Conventional wisdom in Kinshasa says that besides Mobutu and his family only 80 people in the country count. At any one time, 20 of them are ministers, 20 are exiles, 20 are in jail and 20 are ambassadors. Every three months, the music stops and Mobutu forces everyone to change chairs."[31]

The structure of personalist dictatorships varies from one context to the next. It depends largely on the personal preferences of the leader. Leaders in personalist dictatorships may even change the structure of the regime over the course of their time in office.

Since the end of World War II, personalist dictatorships have dotted the landscape of much of the developing world and even parts of the developed world, as the experiences of Spain under Francisco Franco and Portugal under Antonio Oliveira Salazar illustrate. There is no single developing region that has escaped the emergence of personalist dictatorship, though sub-Saharan Africa has seen a larger proportion. This may be due to the fact that it is the poorest region in the developing world: because low levels of economic development are associated with weak institutions,[32] such contexts may facilitate the emergence of personalist rule. It is difficult to disentangle, however, whether weak institutions *cause* personalist dictatorship or are themselves the product of it. Regardless, personalist dictatorships have tended to be more common where levels of economic development are low. With the emergence of personalist dictatorships in more advanced developing countries in recent years, however, such as Turkey, Russia, and Venezuela, this may be changing.

Examples of personalist dictatorship include Malawi under Hastings Banda (1964–1994), the Philippines under Ferdinand Marcos (1972–1986), and Haiti under the Duvaliers (1957–1986).

How Does Authoritarian Regime Type Influence Leaders' Fear of Punishment after Leaving Power?

A number of studies show that authoritarian leaders' expectations about their futures after leaving office influence their behaviors while in power, as discussed in Chapter 4. For the most part, fear of facing a bad fate is associated with quite a bit of bad behavior, including initiating conflict, ratcheting up repression, and clinging to power at all costs.

Authoritarian regimes exhibit systematic differences in terms of how their leaders fare after leaving office.[33] Specifically, in personalist dictatorships, most leaders encounter a bad fate upon their exit from power: 69 percent of personalist leaders are either exiled, imprisoned, or killed after ouster. These numbers are noticeably lower for leaders in other types of authoritarian regimes. Around half of all leaders in monarchic and military dictatorships suffer serious consequences upon leaving power. Leaders in dominant-party dictatorships fare the best, with only about a third (37 percent) facing exile, imprisonment, or death after their exits.

With the exception of military dictatorships, all these numbers are even worse if the leader's overthrow takes down the regime as well. The regime's collapse often signals that enemies of the leader are now in control, whereas its continuance typically means the leader's old allies are. The former should be more likely to try to punish the leader than the latter, and indeed that is what the data show.[34] For this reason, bad fates are more likely when the regime collapses, too.

The evidence therefore suggests that one of the reasons why personalist dictatorships are associated with a host of negative outcomes (many of which will be discussed shortly) is the fact that their leaders are the most likely to fare poorly after leaving power.

What Are the Consequences of Authoritarian Regime Type for Political Outcomes?

Research indicates that authoritarian regimes differ systematically in their policy choices and behaviors. Many of these differences are between personalist dictatorships and other forms of authoritarianism (discussed in Chapter 4), largely because of the absence of checks on the leadership in personalist contexts. That said, occasionally, the differences also are between whether elites come from the military or a dominant party.

First, there is substantial evidence that foreign policy choices are different in personalist dictatorships than they are elsewhere. Among authoritarian regimes, personalist dictatorships are the most likely to initiate conflicts with other states.[35] They are the most belligerent form of dictatorship because they can incite interstate disputes without fearing domestic repercussions should they lose them. Lack of accountability, in other words, leads to riskier behavior. Relatedly, though the well-known democratic peace theory suggests that democracies rarely fight one another, democracies do get into altercations with dictatorships, and these dictatorships are most likely to be personalist.[36] The absence of domestic constraints also makes personalist dictatorships more likely than other forms of authoritarianism to invest in nuclear weapons, as examples of North Korea under the Kim family and Libya under Gaddafi illustrate.[37] It also makes them less likely to engage in cooperative behavior internationally.[38] Personalist dictatorships are the least likely of all dictatorships to sign international agreements, because their leaders have greater policy flexibility.

This same concentration of power, however, makes personalist dictatorships the most vulnerable to collapse in the face of economic sanctions.[39] Leaders in personalist dictatorships are more likely to rely on external sources of revenue to fund their patronage networks, thereby making them more susceptible to overthrow when subject to sanctions. Moreover, because leaders in personalist dictatorships often surround themselves with loyal sycophants to reduce their own risk of ouster, they typically receive bad intelligence. They are therefore not only more likely to start wars, but also more likely to lose them.[40] Leaders in personalist dictatorships intentionally encircle themselves with "yes men" and, consequently, are more likely to receive inaccurate information from their subordinates and make foreign policy errors.[41]

Second, there is evidence that personalist dictatorships make different domestic policy choices than do other forms of authoritarianism. Not surprisingly, research shows that policies are more unstable in personalist dictatorships than elsewhere. Leaders can change policy on a whim because there are no other actors who need to weigh in on choices.[42] As evidence of this, they see more volatile inflation from one year to the next than other dictatorships do; they are also better able to react quickly to exogenous price shocks. In addition, personalist dictatorships are the most likely of all authoritarian regimes to waste foreign aid. Rather than devoting aid toward political liberalization (which is usually its intended purpose), personalist dictatorships direct it toward their narrow group of supporters as a means of extending their hold on power.[43] In other dictatorships, by contrast, leaders rely on larger support groups and, as a result, might anticipate that they have a reasonably good chance of remaining in office after democratization. They are therefore more likely to devote foreign aid to political liberalization, as envisioned. Relatedly, there is also some evidence that the absence of constraints in personalist dictatorships leads to lower levels of economic growth and investment than in other authoritarian regimes.[44] There is evidence as well that they are the most prone to corruption.[45] Because personalist dictatorships are rarely punished for abuses of power, they can engage in corrupt acts as a means of rewarding their small network of supporters.

Third, personalist dictatorships are less susceptible to regime collapse in response to typical threats to their rule than are other dictatorships. For example, personalist dictatorships are less vulnerable to overthrow in the face of economic crises than are other forms of authoritarianism: citizens may suffer when the regime's economy performs poorly, but not the small group of regime supporters.[46] It often takes a full-fledged economic disaster for personalist regimes to encounter destabilizing challenges to their rule. For similar reasons, personalist dictatorships are more resilient to mass protests than are other forms of dictatorship.[47]

Many important political outcomes differ based on whether an authoritarian regime is personalist or not. A number of others, however, depend on whether a dominant party rules the regime or some other group. There is evidence, for example, that dominant-party dictatorships are less repressive than are other forms of dictatorship.[48] Because dominant-party governments are more likely to incorporate a sizable segment of the population into the political process, they are less likely to use repression as a means of influencing the population, instead exerting control through institutional channels. For somewhat similar reasons, dominant-party regimes also experience fewer civil wars than do other types of authoritarian regimes. Their tendency to include large groups of supporters in politics makes them more skilled at preventing grievances from escalating.[49]

Importantly, there are very large differences in leader survival, regime survival, and democratization, based on whether the regime is military or not. Leaders in military dictatorships have far shorter tenures than do those who govern elsewhere: military dictators last around 4 years in office, on average, compared to other dictators, who last around 9 years.[50]

These differences in leader longevity are largely due to the fact that the elite in military dictatorships have access to arms and the skills to use them.[51] Should they wish to oust the leader, it is far easier to do so than in dictatorships, where the elite lack such resources.

Not only are military dictators more vulnerable to overthrow than are other authoritarian leaders, but so are their regimes. Military dictatorships are the shortest lived of all authoritarian regimes, while dominant-party dictatorships are the most long-lasting. Military dictatorships are also the most likely to democratize upon their collapse and personalist dictatorships are the least so. The reasons underlying these differences are explained in detail in Chapter 8.

To summarize, there are very real differences in political outcomes across authoritarian regimes that surface once they are disaggregated. Many of these differences are based on whether dictatorships are personalist or not, but a number of others have to do with whether there is a dominant party or military in government. Taken together, the evidence offered here suggests that lumping authoritarian regimes together into a single category risks obscuring significant differences in their behaviors. This is but one typology that illustrates this; others surely do as well.

What Type of Authoritarian Regime Is Most Common Today?

Figure 5.1 presents the number of authoritarian regimes in power from 1946 to 2010, broken down by regime type.[52] It shows a number of interesting trends. The first is that monarchic dictatorships, which were always relatively rare, have remained so to this day. As of 2010, nearly all these regimes are in the Middle East, including those in Oman, Saudi Arabia, and the United Arab Emirates, with a notable exception being the monarchic dictatorship in Swaziland.

Second, military dictatorships increased in number as the Cold War intensified, but have steadily decreased since. Much

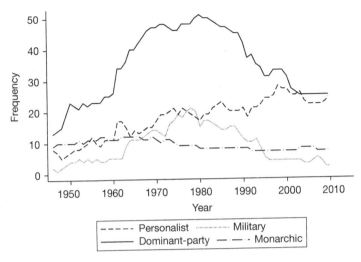

Figure 5.1 Number of authoritarian regimes in power, by type: 1946 to 2010.

of the reason behind the rise of military dictatorships during the Cold War had to do with the United States and Soviet Union supporting these regimes to further their strategic interests at this time. The decline of military dictatorships that occurred subsequently can similarly be tied to both of these superpowers withdrawing their financial backing of these regimes as the Cold War came to its end. As of 2010, military dictatorships make up only a handful of the world's authoritarian regimes, including the regime in Myanmar, which at the time of writing may be in the process of negotiating a transition out of power.[53]

Third, dominant-party dictatorships throughout the period have been the most common form of authoritarian regime. Like military dictatorships, they also rose and fell as the Cold War heated up and simmered. This is largely due to the spread and demise of Communist rule during this period, which lends itself to a dominant-party form of authoritarian governance. As of 2010, only a few Communist dominant-party dictatorships still remain in power, such as those in Laos, China, Cuba, and Vietnam. That said, even with the decline of Communism worldwide, there are more dominant-party dictatorships in office than any other form of authoritarian regime. Examples include the dominant-party regimes in Ethiopia, Singapore, Angola, and Tanzania.

Fourth, throughout the period, personalist dictatorships have steadily increased in number. From 2000 to 2010, they nearly equaled the number of dominant-party dictatorships in power. Should the rise of personalist dictatorship continue, they will become the most common form of authoritarian regime. Examples of contemporary personalist dictatorships include Belarus under Alexander Lukashenko, Uganda under Yoweri Museveni, Chad under Idriss Deby, and Azerbaijan under Ilham Aliyev.

It is difficult to assess why personalist dictatorship is becoming a more frequent form of authoritarian rule. The end of the Cold War can account for some of the decline in dominant-party rule and much of the decline in military rule. The ideology-based regimes of the Cold War (with the Communists on the left and the military juntas primarily on the right) experienced a number of policy failures and were therefore discredited, perhaps paving the way for post-ideological authoritarianism, which is particularly compatible with personalist rule.[54] It is also possible that the emphasis on mimicking democracy—*en vogue* in the post–Cold War period—is easily accomplished with personalist dictatorship.

Regardless of the "whys" behind the rise of personalist dictatorship, all signs indicate it is set to continue. Though systematic codings of regime type only go through 2010, many of the new authoritarian regimes that have come to power since appear to be personalist. Examples include the brief dictatorships in Afghanistan under Hamid Karzai from 2010 to 2014, Ukraine under Viktor Yanukovych from 2012 to 2014, and Sri Lanka under Mahinda Rajapaksa from 2010 to 2015, as well as a few dictatorships still in power at the time of writing, such as the regime of Pierre Nkurunziza in Burundi that began in 2010 upon his consolidation of power around the time of that year's election, that of Salva Kiir Mayardit in South Sudan that began after that country's independence in 2011, and that of Recep Erdogan in Turkey that solidified following his crackdown on the opposition after 2016's failed coup. It is true that not all new dictatorships that have emerged since the start of 2010 fit the strongman mold, such as the military dictatorships in Thailand (which assumed power in 2014 and is still in office at the time of writing) and Mali (in power from 2012 to 2014), but a sizable proportion of them seem personalist in nature. (See Chapter 4 for a discussion of the indicators of personalization—the process of movement toward one-man rule—and some of its political consequences.)

Moreover, many of the world's democracies on the brink of transitioning to dictatorship feature a strongman leader, such as Daniel Ortega of Nicaragua, Rodrigo Duterte of the Philippines, and Viktor Orban of Hungary.[55] I cannot say for certain whether the rise in personalist dictatorship is set to continue in the years to come, but all signs are pointing in that direction.

6

HOW AUTHORITARIAN REGIMES GAIN POWER

How Do Authoritarian Regimes Gain Power?

From 1946 to 2010, 250 new authoritarian regimes came to power. About half of the time (46 percent), these regimes toppled pre-existing authoritarian regimes; just over a quarter of the time (29 percent), they toppled democracies; and the rest of the time, they came to power at the time of independence.

Research identifies seven general ways in which authoritarian regimes gain power: a dynastic family takeover, a coup, an insurgency, a popular uprising, an authoritarianization (i.e., incumbent takeover), a rule change that alters the composition of the ruling group, or a foreign power's imposition.[1]

In the post–World War II period, a coup has been the most common method would-be autocratic groups have used to gain control. It accounts for 46 percent of all authoritarian seizures of power. Examples include the coup that launched the Brazilian military dictatorship to power in 1964, as well as the coup in 1966 in Indonesia that eventually propelled Suharto to power. The former ousted a democracy, while the latter overthrew an authoritarian regime.

Authoritarianization is the second most common method for coming to power, making up 18 percent of all authoritarian seizures of power. These occur when the leadership group comes to power via democratic elections but then uses this position of power to disadvantage and sideline opponents and consolidate control. Examples include Kenya in 1963, when the Kenya African National Union party won competitive elections just before independence but then subsequently implemented de facto one-party rule; Zambia in 1996, when incumbent President Frederick Chiluba signed a constitutional amendment that barred the most viable opposition candidate (Kenneth Kaunda) from contesting the presidency; and Venezuela in 2005, when opposition parties boycotted that year's election following a prolonged government campaign to intimidate and disadvantage them and supporters of President Hugo Chavez won all seats in parliament.[2]

Insurgency and foreign imposition are the next most frequent seizure method, comprising 13 percent and 12 percent of all authoritarian seizures, respectively. Insurgencies are when armed groups battling state forces are victorious and establish an authoritarian government. In this way, they differ from popular uprisings, which are largely unarmed mass demonstrations. An example of an insurgency seizure is the 1975 victory of the People's Movement for the Liberation of Angola in its fight for independence against the Portuguese; another example is the 1994 victory of Paul Kagame and the Rwandan Patriotic Front in its battle with Rwandan government forces and Hutu militia. Foreign impositions are when foreign powers install authoritarian governments typically following a period of occupation. Examples of foreign imposition include the establishment of the East German regime in 1949 (when the Soviet Union transferred administrative authority to the newly formed German Democratic Republic), and the inauguration of the Balaguer regime in the Dominican Republic in 1966 following U.S. occupation.

Popular uprising, a rule change that alters the composition of the ruling group, and armed family takeover make up the remaining ways in which authoritarian regimes assume power (at 5 percent, 4 percent, and 2 percent, respectively). Takeovers via popular uprising are fairly straightforward events.

Examples include the 1979 revolution in Iran that installed the theocracy and the mass protests in Armenia in 1998 that enabled Robert Kocharyan to assume power. Rule changes that alter the composition of the ruling group are less obvious developments. These occur when authoritarian incumbents alter guidelines for behavior (sometimes informally) such that the ruling group is no longer the same. An example is, what occurred in Iraq when Saddam Hussein officially gained control in 1979, transitioning the regime from one in which elites came from the Baathist party to one in which they mainly came from Saddam's personal network. Finally, dynastic family takeovers occur 'when a ruling family officially gains control following independence. An example is, the establishment of the regime in Kuwait in 1961. The al-Sabah family had governed Kuwait under the British protectorate, but officially gained control following independence.

How Does the Type of Seizure of Power Influence What Is to Come?

Some authoritarian regimes seize control via coup, such as Agosto Pinochet's regime in Chile from 1973 to 1989. Others assume control in a subtler fashion via authoritarianization, such as the regime Alberto Fujimori established in Peru in 1992 that lasted until 2000.

How an authoritarian regime gains power is important because it often sets the stage for how politics will work down the road, primarily in terms of the type of group from which leaders and elites will be drawn.

Take the aforementioned examples from Chile and Peru, which represent the two most common ways that dictatorships seize power. In the Chilean instance, the military stormed the Chilean presidential palace and attacked until then-President Salvador Allende took his own life. This led to the establishment of a dictatorship in Chile under the leadership of Pinochet and a military junta. The military's role in the seizure of power paved the way for its subsequent involvement in politics. This is not to say that coups always lead to military dictatorship, but rather that they make it more likely. In Peru, by contrast, Fujimori won free and fair elections in 1990 but closed the legislature in 1992 in an *autogolpe*. The authoritarian regime he established was quite similar in form to the democratic one that he previously governed, apart from the fact that one was authoritarian and the other democratic. Authoritarianizations typically do not lead to a dramatic change in the leadership group, given that they represent power grabs on the part of incumbents. In this instance, Fujimori simply used his position of power to establish personalist rule.

Research suggests that there are patterns between the type of seizure of power and the form of authoritarianism that emerges.[3] Military dictatorships nearly always take power via coup, as the Chilean case exemplifies. Among dominant-party dictatorships, about a third come to power through authoritarianization, another third through insurgency, and another third through either foreign imposition or coup. Not surprisingly, monarchic dictatorships typically stem from a dynastic family takeover, though a number have also emerged from foreign imposition. Lastly, personalist dictatorships have quite varied origins. Forty percent seized power via coup; the bulk of the rest did so either through authoritarianization, foreign imposition, or insurgency.

As these statistics illustrate, the type of seizure of power can give us insight into the form of authoritarianism that will emerge afterward.

How Do Most Authoritarian Regimes Gain Power Today?

Since the end of the Cold War, there have a been a few important changes in terms of how authoritarian regimes form. Figure 6.1 illustrates this. It shows the typical ways that authoritarian regimes have gained control, looking at both the

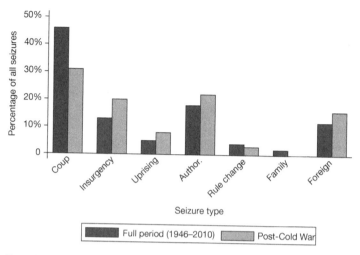

Figure 6.1 How authoritarian regimes seize power.

full post–World War II period and the post–Cold War period exclusively.

There are a number of key things to point out. First, dynastic family takeovers and rule changes that alter the composition of the ruling elite have declined in frequency: there were no dynastic family takeovers and only two rule change seizures. In their place, popular uprisings have increased slightly; they now make up about 8 percent of all authoritarian seizures of power since 1990.

Second, coups have decreased substantially since the end of the Cold War, as discussed in earlier chapters. They currently make up about a third of all authoritarian seizures of power. Though coups are occurring less often than they once did, they are still the most common method through which new dictatorships assume control.

Third, authoritarianizations, insurgencies, and foreign power impositions have each become more common seizure methods in the post–Cold War period, comprising 22 percent, 20 percent, and 16 percent of all authoritarian seizures of power, respectively.

The overall picture that surfaces is that in the post–Cold War era there is no longer a single typical way through which authoritarian regimes seize power.

If we break up seizures of power according to whether they toppled existing authoritarian regimes or democracies, additional trends of interest emerge. Taking a look at the subset of dictatorships that overthrew dictatorships, for example, coups are still the most common method for seizing control (comprising 39 percent of cases), but there has been a dramatic rise in insurgencies since the end of the Cold War in that they now make up a third (33 percent) of all such seizures. Popular uprisings have also become more common; they now comprise 17 percent of all seizures of power in which an authoritarian regime ousts a pre-existing authoritarian regime. These trends suggest that broad-based movements, many of which are violent and protracted, are now the most frequent way through which new dictatorships sprout from existing ones.

If we look instead at authoritarian regimes that overthrew democracies, we see a slightly different picture. As in other contexts, coups have dropped considerably since the end of the Cold War; they are decreasingly a tool of choice for would-be autocratic groups. Though about half of all democracies that fell apart in the post–Cold War era did so via coup, authoritarianizations are on track to outnumber them. They now make up 38 percent of all democratic collapses, and—given events in Turkey, the Philippines, and Bangladesh over the past few years—all signs indicate that they will continue to rise in number. The message that emerges is that democracies are increasingly falling apart through incumbent takeovers.

As a final point, while in the past new authoritarian regimes were far more likely to seize power from a pre-existing dictatorship than a democracy, this, too, is changing. Since the end of the Cold War, 41 percent of all new dictatorships overthrew a democracy, compared to 37 percent that overthrew a dictatorship (the rest took power after the country's independence). This suggests that new dictatorships are increasingly sprouting from democracies, consistent with trends discussed in Chapter 3 indicating a rise in authoritarianism in recent years.[4]

What Is Democratic Backsliding?

Democratic backsliding refers to "changes in the formal political institutions and informal political practices that significantly reduce the capacity of citizens to make enforceable claims upon the government."[5] It is essentially the erosion of democracy.

Democratic backsliding is often set in motion by a series of events that take place across multiple domains, such that there is rarely a single event that signifies it is occurring. Rather, degradations of democracy happen in a number of areas, primarily in terms of the competitiveness of elections, government accountability, and civil and political liberties.[6]

Does Democratic Backsliding Always Mean the Start of an Authoritarian Regime?

Democratic backsliding can lead to the beginning of an authoritarian regime, but not always. Many countries simply experience decreases in "levels" of democracy without actually transitioning to dictatorship.

For example, many observers think Poland has been in the process of democratic backsliding since the Law and Justice Party came to power in 2015.[7] Negative developments include a law that makes it difficult for the Constitutional Tribunal to overturn legislation passed by the legislature, another law that enables the government to hire and fire those in charge of public media outlets, and government efforts to discredit members of the media and academia who challenge its portrayal of events.[8] These occurrences and others are clearly troubling for democracy in Poland, but fall short of signifying a transition to authoritarianism. By most accounts (including my own), Poland is still democratic. As an example, the watchdog organization Freedom House rated Poland "Free" in 2016 despite the declines in respect for civil liberties it documented there that year.[9]

In other instances, of course, democratic backsliding does give way to authoritarianism, such as in Turkey under the leadership of President Recep Tayyip Erdogan. In 2016, the Erdogan government took control of the leading daily newspaper (which supported its opponents), accused academics who opposed its policies of being "treasonous" (causing many to lose their jobs), and pushed through changes to the constitution that gave the president more powers. Importantly, following a failed coup that year, the government initiated a three-month state of emergency that led to the detention or job dismissal of over 15,000 individuals, as well as the closure of a number of media outlets and civil society groups. For these reasons, I no longer consider Turkey democratic, and many others do not either.[10]

To summarize, democratic backsliding always means a deterioration of the quality of democracy, but whether it signifies a transition to authoritarianism as well depends on the severity of what has occurred.

What Is the Difference between Democratic Backsliding and Authoritarianization?

Both democratic backsliding and authoritarianization indicate a movement from more toward less democracy. Democratic backsliding can occur, however, without a country fully crossing the threshold into dictatorship. An example would be Hungary since the ascension to power of Prime Minister Viktor Orban in 2010. Democratic backsliding may or may not mean transition to dictatorship, while authoritarianization by definition guarantees it. Put differently, authoritarianization is one type of democratic backsliding that results in the establishment of dictatorship.

What Are the Telltale Signs of Authoritarianization?

As with democratic backsliding more generally, the gradual nature of authoritarianization can make it difficult to identify. Doing so requires attention to political developments taking place in many arenas. Generally, each event on its own is not sufficient to assert that a country has transitioned to dictatorship; taken together, however, they are. There are exceptions, of course—such as when democratically elected Fujimori of Peru initiated an *autogolpe* that closed down the legislature on April 5, 1992, and marked the start of the authoritarian regime he governed until 2000—but they are rare.

Authoritarianizations typically have in common an effort on the part of incumbents to slowly undermine institutional constraints on their rule, weaken those who oppose them, and sideline and splinter civil society. "Incumbents" in this instance refer to either individual leaders or a group of elites (typically, the upper echelon of a political party).

There are a number of telltale signs of authoritarianization that are typical across cases. The first is the placement of incumbent loyalists in high positions of power, primarily in the judiciary. The purpose of this tactic is to stack key government institutions that could potentially check the power of the governing group with those who support it. By putting allies in the judiciary, incumbents diminish the likelihood that judges will challenge the legality of their choices.

The experience of Venezuela under Chavez illustrates this. In 2004, one of the first red flags signaling Venezuelan democracy was under threat was a law passed in May of that year allowing the government to expand the size of the Supreme Court from 20 to 32 members. The Chavista-led Congress then staffed all the new positions plus five vacancies with supporters of Chavez.[11]

A second indicator of authoritarianization is an attempt to gain control over the media, often by censoring media outlets, seizing power over them, or arresting critical journalists. A free media is a key requirement for democracy to function; citizens must have access to accurate information if they are to effectively evaluate their current and prospective representatives. By engaging in tactics that muzzle the media or ensure that it promotes a pro-government line, incumbents create a narrative that is simultaneously supportive of their rule and critical of those who oppose them.

An example of this is Burundi, where incumbent President Pierre Nkuruniziza carried out an authoritarianization in 2010. When pro-Nkuruniziza groups murdered a number of opponents in September following elections earlier that year, the Burundian media's reporting on these events prompted the director of the national police to hold a press conference warning it not to "interfere" in security issues. Around the same time, the government arrested a number of journalists who criticized it, with many others receiving death threats.[12]

An additional signal of authoritarianization is the manipulation of electoral rules to favor the incumbent. This tactic is geared toward ensuring that the governing group has an easier time winning elections, enabling it to maintain the façade of democracy while disadvantaging the opposition. Simple changes in electoral rules, which dictate how votes are translated into who wins office, can make a large difference in representation, making this a savvy and effective method for amassing power.

As an example, in Benin shortly before its first post-independence election in 1960, the dominant party—the Dahomeyan Unity Party (PDU)—changed the pre-existing electoral rules to a winner-take-all voting system in a single national district, with the additional stipulation that the top two candidates of the party that won would also win the presidency and vice presidency. These changes ensured that the PDU would win not only the top leadership positions, but also full control of the legislature.[13]

A fourth sign of authoritarianization is the passing of a constitutional amendment that empowers the incumbent. The goal of such a move is to legitimate a grab for power. Because the power grab is enshrined in the constitution—and typically agreed upon through a process that at least feigns deliberation—it is easier to paint the move as lawful.

An example comes from Zambia, where in 1996 then-President Frederick Chiluba and the governing Movement for Multiparty Democracy pushed through a constitutional amendment prior to the elections to be held that year. The amendment stipulated that individuals could not seek the presidency if they were born to parents who were not Zambian by birth, thereby prohibiting Chiluba's chief rival, former president Kenneth Kaunda, from running for president because of his partial Malawian heritage.[14]

A fifth indicator of authoritarianization is the use of lawsuits and legislation to sideline civil society and government opponents. The purpose of such efforts is to restrict the public space so that it only includes those who support the government. Because those who are targeted did something "illegal," it is easy for the government to justify punitive actions.

In Turkey under Erdogan, for example, citizens voted in support of a referendum that gave the Erdogan government substantially more constitutional authorities, one of which was expanded control for the State Supervisory Board in its oversight of public and private bodies, including prosecutorial powers.[15] Opponents alleged that the vote was unfair, but regardless, its approval effectively gave the president the ability to police civil society.[16] (The Turkish example also illustrates the aforementioned use of constitutional changes to give the executive greater control.)

These indicators of authoritarianization are, of course, not the ones that exist, but they are among the most frequently seen. Taken together, they result in greater executive authority and a weakening of the institutions necessary for vibrant democracy, which eventually cumulate into the onset of authoritarianism.

Why Are These Indicators of Authoritarianization Important to Be Aware Of?

Though we typically think of democracies falling apart via force, the data indicate that authoritarianizations are on the rise, as discussed earlier in this chapter. If current trends continue, authoritarianizations are set to be the most common way through which democracies collapse. It is therefore important to be aware of what the telltale signs of authoritarianizations are to gain greater awareness of when such modes of democratic breakdown are in the process of occurring. This is particularly true given that authoritarianizations are typically the cumulation of multiple events that occur across a span of time, unlike coups, which generally take place over the course of a single day.

Take the example of Venezuela. In 1998, Chavez won the presidency in free and fair elections and assumed office the following year. Though his tenure was controversial and Venezuelan democracy flawed, Venezuela remained democratic in the years that followed. The situation deteriorated, however, as Chavez's tenure progressed.[17] In 2004, it worsened considerably. That year, the opposition gathered enough signatures to generate a recall referendum. Chavez survived the recall vote, which most observers deemed free and fair. Afterward, however, parliament passed legislation that increased the size of the Supreme Court and enabled judges to be fired by a majority vote. Chavistas controlled the courts by the end of the year. Importantly, the government also published a list of tens of thousands of Venezuelans who had supported the recall petition, many of whom were later fired from their jobs or lost their access to state benefits. Chavez cracked down on the media, in addition, and launched a campaign designed to scare off "anti-revolutionaries." In 2005 (the year in which

I consider Venezuela to have transitioned to authoritarianism), the opposition boycotted legislative elections because of evidence that fingerprint machines were in place that would enable the government to identify who voted against Chavez. Many feared the same type of retribution that happened following the recall vote. On election day, troops were put in place at many polling stations; the contest resulted in Chavista victories across the board.[18]

As this example illustrates, though most observers today concur that Venezuela is a dictatorship, the timing of the transition could be debated given the subtlety of what transpired. For those concerned with global democracy, therefore, appropriately combating or preventing authoritarianization is a difficult task. A first step, however, is knowing the types of events that signal it is en route to happening.

Why Are Authoritarianizations on the Rise?

Coups have historically been the most common means through which democracies have fallen apart, but authoritarianizations are set to outnumber them soon, as mentioned earlier. We have some insight into why coups have declined since the end of the Cold War: Cold War geopolitical dynamics prompted world powers to financially support many militaries in the developing world and, in some cases, back their staging of coups against democratically elected governments; the end of the Cold War, however, led to a withdrawal of this support, as well as laws in a number of countries that deny foreign aid to governments put in power via coup.

Understanding why authoritarianizations have increased in frequency, however, is less straightforward. Part of the reason for the rise of authoritarianizations since the end of the Cold War likely has to do with the fact that they are easier to execute. Coups, for example, are risky endeavors that require careful planning and coordination. About half of coups fail, and their plotters are usually harshly punished afterward.[19]

Authoritarianizations, by contrast, simply require a series of rule and personnel changes that cumulate into a situation in which the opposition can no longer effectively compete for office. They therefore do not generate the same international and domestic backlash on the part of democracy advocates that more overt authoritarian seizures often do, such as coups or insurgencies. Relatedly, greater international acceptance of the democratic model in the post–Cold War era may be putting more pressure on would-be autocratic groups to maintain the façade of democracy, which is more easily accomplished via authoritarianization than more abrupt seizure methods. And because many of these would-be autocratic groups have the support of large sectors of the citizenry, we may be less likely to see citizens speak out against authoritarianization given its gradual nature.

How Does Populist Rhetoric Enable Authoritarianization?

Developments worldwide in the past decade or so suggest that populism is becoming a platform for authoritarianizations, with populist rhetoric among democratically elected leaders serving as a launching pad for transitions to authoritarianism.[20] Populism is not a new phenomenon, of course, and the underlying message it promotes is the same as it was in decades past. What has changed, however, is the method through which aspiring autocrats are using it to ascend to power. Rather than the clean break with democracy of years past, we are now seeing populism used to subtly chip away at it.

There are a few central messages in the populist playbook.[21] The first is that the leader (or leadership group) alone can save the country (which is in need of saving). The idea is that citizens need decisive and strong leadership, and only a visionary executive can solve their country's problems. This message paves the way for authoritarianization because it justifies consolidation of power. Support for increasing the strength of the leadership group, after all, implies support for diminishing the powers of those institutions that could check it. As an example, when Argentines elected Juan Peron president in 1946, his message was that the country "urgently needed a strong and charismatic leader who was able to actually solve the problems."[22] The country later experienced authoritarianization led by Peron in 1951.

A second message is that the traditional political elite (or some other "anti-patriotic" target group) is dangerous and corrupt, the idea being that pre-existing institutions (such as major political parties) are not doing their jobs and cannot handle things. As an example, Venezuela's then-President Chavez stated in 2002, "We must confront the privileged elite who have destroyed a large part of the world."[23] Similarly, one of the slogans promoted during Fujimori's presidential campaign in 1990 in Peru was "a president like you," suggesting that traditional political elites were undesirable candidates.[24] Likewise, in his bid for the presidency in 1994, Alexander Lukashenko of Belarus campaigned heavily on the message that the powers that be were crooked, asserting that he alone would defeat corruption, "which like an all-devouring octopus has ensnared all government organs with its tentacles."[25] Venezuela subsequently transitioned to dictatorship via authoritarianization in 2005, Peru in 1992, and Belarus in 1994.

A third populist message is that the media and/or experts cannot be trusted. Here, the purpose is to discredit sources of information to shed doubt on the veracity of their claims. If the media and experts are not trustworthy, then there is little reason to believe any of the evidence they put forth that is contrary to the government line. Promoting a message that is distrustful of the media and expert insights, therefore, is intended to weaken the ability of citizens to thoughtfully and critically evaluate government policies and performance. Populists present themselves as the "voice of the people," who know the difference between right and wrong intuitively and do not need experts or the media to inform their positions.[26]

All these classic populist messages are antithetical to functional democracy, which is threatened if it relies on a single individual or group to dictate policy as opposed to institutions, if electoral contests are driven by personality rather than structured by political parties, and if voters lack access to a free media and accurate and relevant information for making policy choices.

Even where populism has not given way to a full transition to dictatorship, it has led to democratic degradation in a number of places.[27] In the Philippines, for example, President Rodrigo Duterte used a populist platform during his 2016 bid for office. After gaining control, he launched a brutal crackdown on drugs that killed thousands of civilians, and his assault on the media has been so extensive that the Philippines is now one of the most dangerous countries in the world for journalists.[28] As a result of these developments, the Philippines is currently either on the verge of dictatorship or there already, depending on the observer.[29]

In Hungary as well, Prime Minister Viktor Orban, who came to power in 2010 using a populist message, pushed through electoral rule changes prior to parliamentary elections in 2014, virtually ensuring the victory of his party, Fidesz.[30] He also closed the country's leading newspaper (*Nepszabadsag*) in 2016, after it had exposed a number of Fidesz corruption scandals.[31] International transparency watchdogs have additionally criticized the Orban government for its disproportionate control over the media and advertising outlets, which seriously disadvantages its opponents.[32]

In Nicaragua, too, President Daniel Ortega won free and fair elections in 2006 touting populist themes. In recent years, however, Ortega has carried out a number of actions that have undermined democracy. For example, he put his wife, sons, and daughters in key positions of power; amended the constitution in 2014 so that he could run for a third presidential term; and expelled opposition lawmakers from the National Assembly in 2016.[33]

In sum, though it by no means guarantees it, populist rhetoric lends itself to authoritarianization specifically, and often democratic degradation more generally.[34]

Why Are Today's Authoritarianizations Increasingly a Springboard for Personalist Dictatorship?

The evidence indicates that authoritarianizations are increasingly the process through which would-be autocrats topple democracies, often by featuring populist messages that emphasize consolidation of authority and strong leadership, among other themes. These authoritarianizations, in turn, are increasingly giving way to the most dangerous form of dictatorship: personalist rule.[35]

The data reveal that 44 percent of authoritarianizations led to personalist dictatorship from 1946 to 1999, a number that jumped to 75 percent from 2000 to 2010.[36] This represents a substantial increase. Notable recent examples of this dynamic come from Venezuela under Chavez, Russia under Putin, and Turkey under Erdogan.

Perhaps it is unsurprising that populist-fueled authoritarianizations lead to personalist rule given that so many messages common to populists are exemplified by personalist dictatorship. For example, personalist dictatorships epitomize political systems with strong leadership, which is central to the populist agenda. In addition, leaders install loyalists in key positions of power in personalist dictatorships, something that is consistent with the populist message that is so distrustful of experts. Personalist dictatorships are keen to promote family members and allies to powerful posts as well, which is in line with the populist motto that attacks the traditional political establishment. Personalist dictatorships also create new political parties or movements when they can, which reflects the populist message that pre-existing parties are not fixing citizens' problems.

It is likely for these reasons that today's authoritarianizations, which are themselves on the rise, are increasingly serving as a springboard for personalist rule. Given the negative consequences of personalist dictatorship outlined in earlier chapters, this is a trend that spells trouble for global peace and democracy.

7

STRATEGIES FOR SURVIVAL

What Tools Do Authoritarian Regimes Use to Survive in Office?

All governments confront the difficult task of holding on to office. This is particularly the case for authoritarian governments, which lack electoral legitimacy to defend their positions of power and must contend with the omnipresent threat of overthrow. To address this challenge, authoritarian regimes have two broad tools that they use to defend their rule: repression and co-optation.[1]

These tools have existed as long as authoritarianism itself. As Machiavelli pointed out many centuries ago, for a prince to secure order, "men must be either pampered or crushed."[2] Though the way in which authoritarian regimes use repression and co-optation has changed since Machiavelli's time, they remain the critical means for authoritarian regimes to deter challenges to their rule.

In devising their plan for survival, authoritarian leaders weigh the costs and benefits of both these tools. No study (to my knowledge) has comparatively evaluated the costs authoritarian regimes incur when using them, but most assume that repression is the costlier of the two.[3]

What Is Repression and What Is Its Purpose?

Repression is a defining feature of authoritarian rule. It is defined as "actual or threatened use of physical sanctions against an individual or organization, within the territorial jurisdiction of the state, for the purpose of imposing a cost on the target as well as deterring specific activities."[4] In democracies, governments that repress heavily can be unseated; in authoritarian regimes, by contrast, such acts typically go unpunished. For this reason, authoritarian regimes use repression far more than their democratic counterparts do as a method for maintaining control.[5] In fact, there is no authoritarian regime (to my knowledge) that has governed without reliance on repression at some point while in power.

It is likely for this reason that brutality is so frequently associated with authoritarian governance. One need only think of Saddam Hussein's use of poison gas to kill an estimated 5,000 citizens in the Kurdish village of Halabja in 1988, or his hanging of 17 alleged spies for Israel in a public Baghdad square in 1969 during the Baathist regime that preceded his own.[6] Though these very visible and horrific displays of repression often make news headlines and elicit widespread attention, not all authoritarian regimes are so brutal. That said, even so-called benevolent dictators repress to some degree. For example, while repression under Omar Torrijos in Panama paled in comparison to that under his successor Manuel Noriega, Torrijos' regime still tortured and sometimes murdered activists, journalists, and students during its first few years in office.[7]

The reason authoritarian regimes repress is to try to lessen perceived threats to their rule. The idea is that by removing their challengers, silencing them, or preventing them from organizing, it will be easier for such regimes to maintain control. Of course, if doing this were so easy, no authoritarian regime would ever encounter a viable opposition group. Repression can be expensive to execute and requires a government with the capacity to do so.[8] Moreover, it can backfire.

The use of indiscriminate repression has the potential to elicit a backlash against the regime, strengthening opposition to it and triggering popular unrest.[9] Though authoritarian regimes have to rely on repression to some extent to deal with inevitable opposition to their rule, they must be careful in terms of how they do so.

What Are the Different Ways in Which Authoritarian Regimes Repress and How Is This Measured?

Repression comes in many forms, which can be grouped into two broad types: high-intensity repression and low-intensity repression.[10] These types of repression differ both in terms of the target of the repressive act and the type of violence used.

High-intensity repression refers to overt acts of violence, which typically target well-recognized individuals or groups. Examples include mass killings of protestors and assassinations of opposition leaders.[11] The government's killing of hundreds of student demonstrators in Tiananmen Square in China in 1989 qualifies as high-intensity repression, as does the murder of protestors in Uzbekistan in 2005 at the hands of security services. High-intensity repression is easily observable, both for domestic and international audiences, and difficult for authoritarian governments to fully cover up.

Even though it is highly visible, measuring high-intensity repression can be more difficult than one would expect because perpetrating governments have good reason to conceal their activities and lie about the number of individuals involved. Measures of high-intensity repression are therefore far from perfect.[12] They can give us a glimpse into patterns of behaviors across governments, however. One of the more common ways that researchers measure high-intensity repression is by looking at personal integrity violations, which are government activities that target an individual's integrity (as in directly threatening the individual's life), including mass killings and torture.[13] Cross-national measures of political integrity violations include the Political Terror Scale (PTS) and Cingranelli and Richards' Physical Integrity Rights Index (CIRI).[14]

Low-intensity repression, by contrast, is subtler in nature and often has a broader target (i.e., the opposition in general). Examples include surveillance of opposition activities, the use of lawsuits against opponents, and short-term detainments of activists and journalists.[15] China's use of sophisticated methods for monitoring the Internet to spy on its citizens classifies as low-intensity repression; Singapore's practice of using defamation lawsuits to silence its opponents does as well. Low-intensity repression is less likely to attract attention not only because it is understated, but also because it is often a series of small, individual incidents as opposed to a single, large-scale event. Further complicating matters, the government may outsource it and make other groups (such as paramilitary organizations) do the dirty work.

Low-intensity repression is perhaps more difficult to measure than high-intensity repression because it is so subtle and varied in form. There are myriad ways in which governments can carry out low-intensity repression, depending on levels of creativity. Measures of low-intensity repression, for this reason, typically focus on one specific method. The most common way that researchers have measured it is by looking at empowerment rights restrictions, which are government efforts to limit (e.g., arrest, sanction, or ban) expression, association, assembly, and beliefs.[16] The primary cross-national measure of this is Freedom House's civil liberties score, which captures "freedoms of expression and belief, associational and organizational rights, rule of law, and personal autonomy from the state."[17]

How Does Repression Vary across Authoritarian Regimes?

All authoritarian regimes repress to some degree, but some more than others and in different ways. For example, among post–World War II dictatorships, every single regime has restricted empowerment rights in one way or another and all but three have violated physical integrity rights at some point while in office.[18]

That said, there are systematic differences in repressive activities across authoritarian regimes based on type.[19] Specifically, personalist dictatorships rely more heavily on repression of empowerment rights than do other forms of authoritarianism, while military dictatorships are the most likely authoritarian regime type to repress physical integrity rights. Importantly, the evidence suggests that dominant-party dictatorships are the least repressive form of dictatorship, taking both types of repression into consideration.

The literature asserts that dominant-party dictatorships repress less than other dictatorships do because they feature more of the characteristics of democracies thought to reduce repression, primarily the incorporation of a greater slice of the population in the political process.[20] Because dominant-party dictatorships are more likely to provide an arena in which public expression about the regime can take place, they have other means of influencing citizens at their disposal beyond coercion.

How Does Repression Influence Authoritarian Regime Survival?

The purpose of repression is to help governments maintain power, yet there is surprisingly little research on whether this tactic actually works. As one scholar wrote in 2007, "One explanation for state repression is that authorities use it to stay in power, but the literature contains not one systematic investigation of this proposition."[21] Part of the challenge in investigating this relationship is disentangling whether it is repression that increases the regime's strength or vice versa. It could very well be true that those dictatorships that are powerful enough to repress in the first place are going to be the most long-lasting.

Though there is no study (to my knowledge) that examines how repression influences authoritarian regime survival, there is research on its influence on authoritarian leader survival. The evidence indicates that dictators are wise to repress: the more repressive the dictator, the lower the risk of the dictator's overthrow.[22] At the same time, dictators who face a high chance of losing power are likely to respond by increasing levels of repression.

To summarize, we do not know whether repression actually prolongs the survival of authoritarian regimes, the purpose that it is assumed to fulfill. We can infer, however, that by increasing the survival prospects of individual leaders, it lengthens the amount of time that the regimes they lead stay afloat as well.

How Has the Use of Repression in Authoritarian Regimes Changed over Time?

Contemporary authoritarian regimes differ from those of the past in terms of how they repress. Rather than using brute force to maintain control, today's authoritarian regimes use strategies that are subtler and more ambiguous in nature to silence, deter, and demobilize opponents. Doing so serves a number of purposes. It attracts less attention, enables them to plausibly deny a role in what occurred, makes it difficult for opponents to launch a decisive response, and helps the regime feign compliance with democratic norms of behavior.

Indicators of this evolution in the use of repression in dictatorships are apparent across a variety of domains.[23] For one, though in the past most authoritarian regimes used groups overtly tied to the regime to carry out repression, post–Cold War authoritarian regimes are more likely to turn to nominally independent actors to do so. In Iran, for example, the Basij (a voluntary paramilitary group) spearheaded much of the crackdown against protestors that occurred after the 2009 presidential election. This tactic enables the regime to deny that any bloodshed occurred at the hands of official state actors and direct blame elsewhere.

Moreover, rather than simply arresting opponents to silence them, contemporary authoritarian regimes are likely to adopt a more understated approach, such as filing a legal suit against them. Alexander Lukashenko of Belarus, for example, used a criminal libel suit to silence regime opponent Pavel Marozau, who had written cartoons criticizing the government's performance.[24] Singapore under the People's Action Party is notorious for using this tactic, as mentioned earlier, which it leverages to bankrupt opponents. After losing the suit (which they nearly always do), opponents must pay hundreds of thousands in damages, eventually sapping them of all their financial resources.[25] Other similarly subtle tactics include filing regulatory infractions against opposition organizations, such as breaches of health and safety rules, and issuing travel bans on opposition leaders. The purpose of such efforts is to make the regime appear as if it is tolerant of dissent as opposed to brutal and ruthless.

In addition, while in the past authoritarian regimes used overt censorship to keep critics quiet and fractured, those of today are instead allowing opponents to operate in an ostensibly freer space while using creative strategies to closely surveil them. In Uganda, for example, Yoweri Museveni's regime used the malware program FinFisher to stay abreast of real-time communications taking place between key opposition leaders during post-election protests.[26] And in Russia, a pro-Putin think tank created a software program that enables the regime to predict protests through monitoring of social media.[27] Sophisticated techniques such as these enable regimes to track the activities of their opponents and gather information about their intentions to keep them demobilized without having to resort to overt censorship.

This evolution in the use of repression in authoritarian regimes helps to explain why traditional indicators of repression have shown a decline over time in their use.[28] It is not that today's dictatorships no longer repress, but rather that they are doing so differently than in the past.

What Is Co-Optation and What Is Its Purpose?

Authoritarian regimes also use co-optation to maintain power, though they vary considerably in the extent to which they rely on it and how. Co-optation is defined as the intentional extension of benefits to potential challengers in exchange for their loyalty.[29] A classic example is the maintenance of clientele networks, which distribute goods and services to select individuals in return for their political support. The purpose of co-optation is to persuade other key actors not to exercise their "power to obstruct."[30]

There are a number of reasons why co-optation is a useful strategy for dictatorships. First, it can deter defections from both the inner circle and lower-level regime supporters. If regime allies do well under the current regime, they should be less likely to withdraw support for it. This assessment seems obvious, but it is magnified by the very real possibility that such individuals will fare worse under the regime's successor. In this way, co-optation gives regime allies a vested interest in the regime's survival and creates a powerful motive for them to support its continuation.[31]

Co-optation is also effective because it can divide potential opponents to the regime over whether to "accept" the benefit the regime is offering. This protects the regime by making opposition coordination more difficult.[32] For example, allowing opposition political parties to compete in elections is one form of co-optation. Though this is a perk for aspiring politicians, it also has the potential to fracture the opposition given that some may prefer to boycott the election instead.

Another reason co-optation is a valuable survival strategy is that it can decrease the likelihood that small episodes of unrest, which are common but rarely destabilizing in dictatorships, will gain momentum.[33] If broad swaths of the population are disgruntled, such minor events have greater potential to steam-roll into threatening mass opposition movements. Spreading spoils to choice sectors of the population, however, can prevent this from occurring by reducing overall levels of societal dissatisfaction.

Relatedly, whereas news that an authoritarian regime has engaged in repression can fuel the fire of the opposition and trigger a popular backlash, news of an act of co-optation does not bring with it this risk. Co-optation is therefore a "safer" strategy in many ways than repression is.[34]

It is important to note, however, that co-optation is not risk free. By giving potential regime opponents something they value, co-optation can empower the very individuals the regime seeks to appease. Though the targets of co-optation are supposed to remain loyal in exchange for the benefits they receive, there is always the risk that they will leverage such resources to jump ship. Once individuals have received the transfer, there is nothing to guarantee they will not use it to develop and strengthen their own coalitions.[35] Co-optation can therefore be risky for dictatorships because its targets can potentially leverage received benefits toward undermining the regime.[36]

What Are the Different Ways in Which Authoritarian Regimes Use Co-Optation?

The use of co-optation in authoritarian regimes is quite varied. Some acts of co-optation are directed toward the regime elite, others toward members of the opposition, others toward specific sectors of the masses, and others toward all three. Because allies of the regime today can easily transform into its opponents tomorrow, regime supporters are typical targets of co-optation. Opponents whose support can be bought are as well. For example, authoritarian regimes that draw support from a specific ethnic group may co-opt co-ethnics to secure their loyalty to the regime; they may also co-opt rival ethnic groups in an effort to dissuade them from seeking the regime's overthrow.

The benefits distributed via co-optation range from economic perks, such as newly paved roads or preferential tax rates, to political privileges, such as influence over the direction of policy or control over the selection of personnel to staff government posts. The transfer of such benefits can occur informally (via patronage networks) or through official institutional channels.

Methods of co-optation in dictatorships are wide-ranging. Scholars have highlighted, in particular, the use of political institutions as co-optation tools in authoritarian regimes. A regime-affiliated political party, for example, mobilizes popular support for the regime and provides a vehicle for distributing the spoils of office.[37] In this way, it gives party members something at stake in the regime's survival, diminishing the likelihood that they will devote their efforts instead to subvert the regime. Similarly, authoritarian legislatures serve a co-optation function. They offer an arena in which key political actors can negotiate deals and make policy concessions.[38] This is particularly true in *partisan legislatures,* or those in which members of the opposition are given representation. Such legislatures broaden the support base of the regime and diminish the chance of overthrow by functioning as a means for integrating potential opponents into the system.[39] Elections in dictatorships can also work to co-opt aspiring politicians.[40] In holding elections and dictating the rules regarding who can compete in them, authoritarian regimes create "divided structures of contestation" between those who are barred from running for office and those who are not.[41] Those allowed to seek office—and particularly those who win seats—become participants in the regime and subsequently develop vested interests in its survival.

There are additional vehicles for co-optation beyond political institutions, of course. Public employment opportunities can serve as a type of co-optation, for example. There is evidence that in China the Chinese Communist Party (CCP) co-opts ethnic minority groups (a major political threat to its rule) by disproportionately creating public jobs in minority-dominant provinces.[42] Similarly, in the most recent Argentine military dictatorship, the regime bought the loyalty of senior officers by letting them run state-owned enterprises.[43] Co-optation can also come in the simple form of goods and cash. As an illustration, in the Soviet Union the regime allocated cars (a scarce resource at the time) as a means of securing political loyalties to Stalin.[44] In Mexico as well, the Institutional Revolutionary Party (PRI) regime's use of cash transfers to reward political elites was commonplace. As one PRI politician stated, "A politician who stays poor is poor at politics."[45]

As these examples demonstrate, there are many ways in which authoritarian regimes co-opt supposed allies and suspected opponents. Methods of co-opting such individuals are limitless where regimes are creative.

How Does Co-Optation Vary across Authoritarian Regimes?

Most authoritarian regimes use a variety of co-optation tools as part of their survival strategy. Though there are no systematic studies, to my knowledge, that examine how authoritarian regimes differ in their reliance on co-optation, a few broad trends can be pointed out. [46]

First, though nearly all authoritarian regimes rely on informal co-optation—as in patronage distribution—to buy political support, personalist dictatorships are perhaps the most notorious for doing so. In the Philippines under Ferdinand Marcos, for example, the regime "came to be characterized almost exclusively by patronage networks and cronyism."[47] In personalist dictatorships, political institutions are typically weak, making it difficult for the regime to use formal channels to transfer the perks of power to supporters. For this reason, it is common for them to operate patronage networks to distribute rents and secure the loyalty of political elites.[48] The evidence is consistent with this: rates of government consumption as a share of GDP (a proxy for patronage distribution) are higher in personalist dictatorships than in other forms of authoritarianism. [49] Personalist dictatorships can afford such a co-optation strategy because they usually do not need a large network of supporters to stay in power. Their support coalition is typically narrower than it is in other dictatorships, such that it is more feasible to co-opt key actors by informally handing out favors. Personalist dictatorships may use other methods of co-optation as well, but they are particularly likely to rely on the distribution of patronage through informal networks as a means of securing political loyalties.

Second, while it is common for all forms of dictatorship to delegate control over state-run businesses as a means of co-opting key political actors, military dictatorships are especially fond of this tactic. Military dictatorships are less likely than civilian-led dictatorships to feature political parties and, as such, often resort to other state organizations as a vehicle for co-optation. Specifically, they frequently allow members of the military (whose loyalty they must secure to stay in office) to take charge of state enterprises and reap the financial benefits that such control allots. In Thailand, for example, the military junta "stopped short of an outright seizure of the nation's 56 state-owned companies" after coming to power in a coup in 2014.[50] In Myanmar as well, the military junta profits from the wide array of state-owned enterprises there; those that have been privatized are in the hands of two military-controlled business conglomerates.[51] The experience of Latin America provides additional evidence of this behavior. From the 1930s to the 1980s, military rule brought with it military entrepreneurship, or the military's "ownership, management, or stakeholding of economic enterprises."[52] Military dictatorships are certainly not the only type of authoritarian regime to use profits from state businesses as a tool of co-optation, but their patterns of behavior suggest that they are particularly inclined to do so.

Lastly, while many authoritarian regimes rely on a support party to bolster their rule, dominant-party dictatorships are especially likely to use the party as a means of co-opting ambitious and active politicians. Because the party is organizationally strong in such regimes, it is an efficient institution for rewarding and attracting supporters. Dominant-party dictatorships can use access to party posts as a way of capturing the support of those with a vocation for politics.[53] At the mass level, party membership is a way for the regime to distribute small perks to ordinary citizens and give them a stake in the regime's survival. In China, for example, the regime mobilizes low-level party members to help candidates in local elections and lobby on behalf of specific leaders. In doing so, such individuals gain a sense of political efficacy and the belief that they are influencing policy.[54] Elsewhere, dominant parties have distributed rents to ordinary citizens who voted for them, a particularly effective method for "trapping" poor voters into backing the regime because their livelihoods are dependent on such transfers.[55] At the elite level, high-level positions in the party bring with them access to the fruits of office and, in some instances, policy influence. Because elites reap such rewards while the party is in power, they are less likely to defect and try to unseat it. [56] For this reason, "cooptation rather than exclusion is the rule" in dominant-party dictatorships.[57]

How Does Co-Optation Influence Authoritarian Regime Survival?

Distributing benefits to potential challengers is a simple way for an authoritarian regime to maintain power. By giving individuals something they value and would like to continue to receive, dictatorships can deter such individuals from seeking their overthrow and, in many instances, give them vested interests in the regime's survival. When effective, co-optation deters its targets from devoting their energies toward seeking the regime's overthrow and instead incentivizes them to work to keep it afloat.

Resources for co-optation, however, are not infinite. Co-optation can therefore help authoritarian regimes stay in office, but only so long as they can continue to keep it up. It is also not a risk-free strategy, as mentioned earlier. In co-opting potential challengers, authoritarian regimes are empowering the very individuals whose defection they fear.

Surely, some types of co-optation are riskier for authoritarian regimes than others, and some more difficult to maintain. There is little research, however, on the effectiveness of co-optation for authoritarian survival based on the co-optation instrument.

Those studies that do evaluate the impact of co-optation on the survival of dictatorships look at the effect of political institutions specifically. They find that dictatorships that feature political institutions, such as political parties, legislatures, and elections, last longer in office than those that do not.[58] Though the evidence tying these types of political institutions of co-optation with greater authoritarian regime durability is fairly robust, establishing the direction of causality is difficult. It is possible, for example, that "stronger" authoritarian regimes are better able to create these types of institutions in the first place.[59] Regardless, authoritarian regimes that feature such institutions typically govern for longer than their institution-free counterparts.

How Has the Use of Co-Optation in Authoritarian Regimes Changed over Time?

Since World War II, authoritarian regimes have co-opted potential challengers through tried-and-true tactics, such as reliance on patronage networks to divvy out the spoils of office. Over time, however, they have broadened the ways in which they use co-optation. Rather than solely relying on traditional methods of co-optation to secure loyalty, contemporary authoritarian regimes are expanding the methods by which they co-opt potential challengers in innovative ways.[60] Most of these new methods draw from the norms and institutions we typically see in democracies, but are then adapted to meet the survival purposes of the regime.

For one, we are seeing an increasing number of dictatorships use political institutions to co-opt key actors (evidence of which is offered at the end of this chapter). Parties, elections, and legislatures are the typical political institutions of choice, but today's authoritarian regimes have enlarged this list to include others as well. In Russia, for example, Putin created the Public Chamber in 2005 to co-opt key actors. The chamber is a consultative forum made up of civil society representatives who voice their views on legislation and policy issues.[61] Political institutions such as this give activists an official place where they can weigh in on the needs and interests of ordinary citizens, but with the regime firmly in control of the narrative.[62]

Beyond political institutions, there are a multitude of other creative ways in which today's authoritarian regimes are co-opting potential challengers. In Singapore, for example, the government created REACH—Reaching Everyone for Active Citizenry@Home—a center where citizens can electronically give feedback to the government on key issues.[63] Such a project enables the regime to not only collect information about citizen preferences, but also make citizens feel that it is attentive to their needs. Dictatorships in a number of places, such as China, Kazakhstan, Belarus, and Cuba, have even established government-organized nongovernmental organizations (referred to as GONGOs), which are essentially fake civil society organizations staffed by regime allies.[64] The existence of these organizations makes the regime appear welcoming to civil society, while stifling true dissent.[65]

These are but a few examples of the variety of ways in which today's authoritarian regimes have broadened how they co-opt key political actors. Many of these new methods more closely align contemporary dictatorships with democracies in form, but—importantly—not in substance. This is in line with the general trend of post–Cold War authoritarian regimes mimicking democracies to bolster their survival.[66]

What Is the Relationship between Co-Optation and Repression?

Most scholars agree that authoritarian regimes rely on some combination of co-optation and repression as part of their survival strategy. Less is known, however, about how they balance their use of these tactics. Though research in this area is limited, there is evidence of an inverse relationship in some domains. Specifically, institutional co-optation leads to decreased reliance on the repression of empowerment rights.[67] When dictatorships feature multiple political parties and a legislature, it is easier for them to identify their most threatening opponents, both by helping them monitor the popularity of regime officials (who could potentially defect) and by drawing potential opposition members out of hiding and into state institutions.[68] Because the regime has better information about the specific individuals who pose the greatest threat to its survival, it can simply target these individuals in its use of repression and relax restrictions on speech and assembly rights, which often generate popular opposition. As Vladimir Milov, an opposition leader in Russia, stated, "They [dictators] stay away from too much pressure on the general public. They prefer a very focused repression against a few people who are active in proclaiming opposition feeling."[69]

To summarize, while there is evidence suggesting that increased co-optation decreases one specific type of repression, additional research is needed to better understand this relationship.

Are Today's Authoritarian Regimes More Durable Than Those of the Past?

Today's authoritarian regimes have evolved in terms of how they use the central survival tools at their disposal: repression and co-optation. In terms of repression, they are increasingly shying away from overt and highly visible forms of coercion and turning to subtler techniques that are less likely to spark outrage and condemnation. And in terms of co-optation, they are expanding the range of methods they use to co-opt potential challengers, often in ways that strategically imitate the institutions and norms we see in democracies.

Part of the reason behind this evolution lies in the prioritization of democracy in the global arena since the end of the Cold War. Increased pressure, both from international and domestic audiences, to adopt democracy has incentivized dictatorships to feign that they are conforming to it.

At the same time, there are also indications that contemporary authoritarian regimes have adapted their tactics in these ways because doing so is in their interest. They have "learned" that using strategies such as innovative co-optation and ambiguous repression will help them survive in office.[70] For example, pseudo-democratic institutions not only help authoritarian regimes mimic democracy, but they also help them maintain power by co-opting potential challengers. Looking at Figure 7.1, the percentage of dictatorships that feature a legislature and regular elections (at least every six years) in which multiple parties compete has increased over time, and with it the median number of years that the typical dictatorship remains in power.[71] Research examining some of the new survival techniques that authoritarian regimes tells a similar

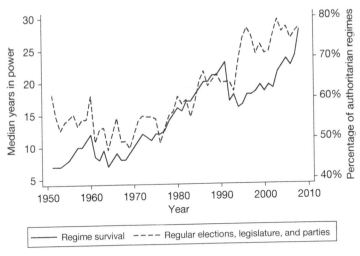

Figure 7.1 Pseudo-democratic institutions and regime durability: 1951 to 2008.

story: dictatorships that have evolved in the aforementioned ways have longer survival rates than do their retrograde counterparts.[72]

The evidence therefore suggests that today's authoritarian regimes are more durable than their predecessors. This enhanced durability is likely due to nuanced changes in the central strategies they use to stay in power, most of which make them look more like democracies than the regimes of years past.

8

HOW AUTHORITARIAN REGIMES FALL

How Do Authoritarian Regimes Fall?

Given the persistent centrality of notorious dictatorships to the foreign policy agendas of many of the world's states, identifying the vulnerabilities of authoritarian regimes is of fundamental importance. One way to gain insight into these vulnerabilities is to examine how authoritarian regimes fall.

From 1946 to 2014, 239 authoritarian regimes fell from power. Research identifies seven ways in which they have done so (six of which roughly mirror the seven ways they have historically seized power discussed in Chapter 6): a coup, an election, a popular uprising, an insurgency, a rule change that alters the composition of the ruling group, a foreign power's imposition, and state dissolution.[1]

Coup is the most common means through which dictatorships collapse, representing a third (33 percent) of all authoritarian regime failures. An example is the 1971 coup General Idi Amin led in Uganda that toppled the dictatorship of Milton Obote. Though many Ugandans rejoiced at the news of Obote's ouster, Amin's behavior soon thereafter gave pause to such optimism, including his dissolution of parliament and murder of hundreds of military officers allied with Obote's region.[2]

The second most frequent way that authoritarian regimes fall is via elections, which make up about a quarter (28 percent) of all authoritarian regime failures. When dictatorships leave power through elections, it is because incumbents either did not run, having already decided to step down; or they ran in elections, lost, and subsequently honored the results.[3] As an example, the Sandinista regime in Nicaragua stepped down in 1990 after losing competitive elections that year. Though there were initial concerns that the Sandinistas would not accept the opposition's surprise victory, incumbent President Daniel Ortega stated soon afterward that he would "obey the popular mandate coming out of the vote."[4]

Popular uprising is the third typical way that authoritarian regimes collapse, accounting for 18 percent of all authoritarian regime failures. An example may be found in the 1979 Iranian revolution, in which months of violent mass protests ultimately forced the Shah to flee to Egypt and led to calls for the return of Ayatollah Ruhollah Khomeini from his exile in France. Soon after returning to Iran, Khomeini declared the country an Islamic republic and set the stage for the establishment of the theocratic regime that governs Iran to this day. (Though popular uprising is a common mode of authoritarian regime collapse, it is important to note the infrequency with which such events are successful. For example, only about 10 percent of all major anti-government revolts in authoritarian regimes actually topple them.[5])

Together, coup, elections, and popular uprising comprise the bulk (79 percent) of authoritarian regime modes of exit. Most of the rest occur through an insurgency or a rule change that alters the composition of the ruling group (8 percent and 7 percent, respectively). Examples of insurgencies come from Cuba, where in 1959 insurgent forces led by Fidel Castro defeated the dictatorship of Fulgencio Batista after six years of fighting, and Somalia, where in 1991 rebel forces toppled strongman ruler Siad Barre, ushering in a period of more than two decades during which no single group exerted control over a majority of the country's territory.[6] Rule changes that alter the composition of the ruling elite occur either when authoritarian incumbents change electoral rules in ways that enable broader actors to compete in elections (thereby changing the set of actors that could control policy) or when a new incumbent changes the rules that define the regime after assuming control. An example of the former is Spain's passing of the Political Reform Law in 1976 at the tail end of the Franco regime, which introduced universal suffrage and paved the way for free and fair elections held the following year. An example of the latter is Madagascar's transition in 1975 from a collective military dictatorship to one with a civilian-military base of support. The military selected Vice Admiral Didier Ratsiraka to the leadership post that year. Ratsiraka subsequently changed the identity of the group from which key political actors were chosen by using a referendum to establish the Second Republic and creating a political party (the Vanguard of the Malagasy Revolution).[7]

The remaining ways in which authoritarian regimes fall are through a foreign power's imposition and state dissolution (making up 4 percent and 2 percent of all failures, respectively). Examples of a foreign power toppling an authoritarian regime include the U.S. invasions of Panama (which led to the ouster of strongman Manuel Noriega in 1989), Afghanistan (which removed the Taliban regime in 2001), and Haiti (which forced the governing military junta to step down in 1994). State dissolution occurs when the state the authoritarian regime governs ceases to exist, either because it splits into multiple states or is incorporated into an existing state. The first instance occurred in 1991, when the USSR disintegrated after decades of Communist rule; the second occurred in Vietnam in 1975, when Communist troops took over Saigon, putting an end to the authoritarian regime governing South Vietnam and ending its existence as a distinct state.

How Do Most Authoritarian Regimes Fall Today?

Since the end of the Cold War, there have been a few key changes in terms of how authoritarian regimes collapse, most of which are consistent with trends in authoritarian regime dynamics identified elsewhere in this book. These are shown in Figure 8.1, which plots the various ways that dictatorships have fallen, both in the full post–World War II period and exclusively since the end of the Cold War.

Importantly, while coup, elections, and popular uprising still make up the bulk (71 percent) of all authoritarian regime exits in the post-1990 period, their relative frequencies are markedly different. Elections have displaced coups as the most common way in which dictatorships end: 39 percent of all authoritarian regime failures currently occur via electoral processes. Most of these transitions lead to democratization, which is not surprising given that they usually occur because authoritarian incumbents allow them to. This is largely due to the increase in democratizations worldwide that occurred in the aftermath of the Cold War.

Exits via popular uprising have increased a bit since the end of the Cold War. They now make up more than a fifth

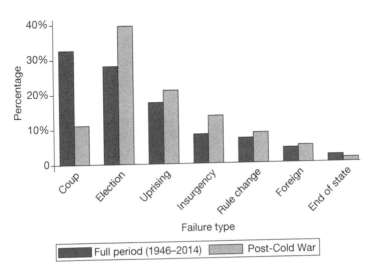

Figure 8.1 How authoritarian regimes fall.

(21 percent) of all authoritarian regime failures. This is consistent with evidence showing that authoritarian leaders are more vulnerable to people-powered movements now than they were in the past.[8]

At the same time, overthrows through coup have decreased considerably in recent decades, such that they now represent only 11 percent of all authoritarian regime failures. This is unsurprising given global declines in the number of coups in the post–Cold War era, discussed in Chapters 4 and 6.

Other forms of authoritarian regime exit have changed only slightly since 1990. Insurgency, a rule change that alters the composition of the ruling group, and a foreign power's imposition are each now more common, but not by much. Rates of state dissolution have remained about constant.

Taken together, the general picture to emerge is that authoritarian regimes are now more vulnerable to mass-based challenges to their rule than they were during the Cold War, when military coups posed the greatest survival threat. This is in line with patterns seen in authoritarian leader exits, covered in Chapter 4.

Do Coups Always Signal the End of an Authoritarian Regime?

Coups are efforts "by the military or other elites within the state apparatus to unseat the sitting executive using unconstitutional means."[9] The goal is nearly always to force a change in the leadership, but often coup plotters have larger ambitions and seek more serious political change as well. In fact, about two-thirds (63 percent) of all coups in dictatorships lead to the collapse of the regime. At the same time, this also means that about a third of all coups do not.[10] The data indicate, in other words, that coups do not necessarily signal regime change, and we cannot anticipate that they do.

Though the survival of a regime following a coup may seem puzzling, in some authoritarian regimes coups are simply the method of choice for changing the leadership. Such "leader-shuffling" coups are particularly common in military dictatorships, where officers seek to replace one military dictator with another and find a coup to be the easiest way to do so.[11] Examples include the coups in 1970 and 1971 during the Argentine military dictatorship that governed from 1966 to 1973, as well as the coups in 1982 and 1983 in the Guatemalan military dictatorship that ruled from 1970 to 1985. In each instance, the coup ousted the junta leader, but without changing the group that could choose leaders and influence policy.

With the decline in military dictatorship, however, leader-shuffling coups have declined as well. Since the end of the Cold War, only about a fifth (18 percent) of all coups in authoritarian regimes amount to simple leadership changes; the vast majority take down the regime, too. Even so, we cannot assume that all coups signal regime failure.

How Does Authoritarian Regime Type Affect the Chance of Regime Failure?

Systematic differences exist across authoritarian regimes in their propensity for collapse, based on type.[12] Figure 8.2 shows the average number of years authoritarian regimes govern, based on regime type. Military dictatorships are the most fragile of all dictatorships, ruling for an average of 7 years. Dominant-party dictatorships are the most long-lasting form of dictatorship, governing for an average of 26 years. Personalist dictatorships are in the middle; they last in office for an average of 11 years. Consistent with the message at the end of Chapter 7 that today's dictatorships are more durable than those of the past, all three types of authoritarian regime have seen their average survival rates go up in the post–Cold War period.

Military dictatorships are most vulnerable to regime failure due to the unique interests of the governing group. As members of the military, elites in these regimes prioritize the survival of the military as an institution. The greatest threat to their rule, therefore, is the military splitting into competing

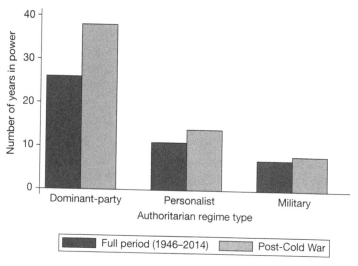

Figure 8.2 Average authoritarian regime duration, by type.

factions and the outbreak of civil war. For this reason, elite splits, which are common in all authoritarian regimes, are particularly destabilizing for military dictatorships. When rivalries or factions within the elite intensify, these regimes often leave power of their own volition. The repercussions for doing so are often not too serious, given that most members of the regime can simply return to the barracks with their careers intact. Military dictatorships therefore carry within them "the seeds of their own destruction," and often last only a few years in office.[13]

In dominant-party dictatorships, by contrast, the governing group has very different motivations. Like democratic politicians, elites in the party prioritize holding office. If the party were to fall from power, most would be out of a job. This gives party elites—even those that oppose the leadership—a strong incentive to stick with the regime rather than try to undermine it. All are better off with the party in office. Moreover, because strong parties typically feature clear (even if informal) rules for handling leadership succession,

dominant-party dictatorships are less vulnerable to collapse in the face of leadership turnover. Only about a quarter
(26 percent) of dominant-party dictatorships fall from power
when their leaders do, compared to about half (56 percent)
of military dictatorships and a majority (71 percent) of personalist dictatorships. For these reasons, dominant-party
dictatorships are substantially more durable than other forms
of authoritarianism.

Personalist dictatorships are more short-lived than
dominant-party dictatorships, but less fragile than military
dictatorships. As in other authoritarian regimes, factions are
common in personalist dictatorships, yet most of the time opposing sides have "strong reasons to continue supporting the
regime and the leader."[14] Personalist elites are substantially
safer with the regime in power than with the alternative. Unlike
elites in dominant-party dictatorships who may be able to compete in elections should the regime fall, the post-regime fate of
elites in personalist dictatorships is particularly dire. Their futures are often closely linked with those of their leaders, who
are frequently punished after leaving power for their actions
while still in it. This gives personalist elites a strong incentive
to continue to back the regime, even if they are displeased with
it. As such, personalist dictatorships typically last longer in office than do military dictatorships. At the same time, personalist dictatorships are particularly likely to collapse in the face
of a leadership transition (as indicated earlier). With hollowed
institutions, they lack the framework for managing leadership
succession. Should the leader leave power, the regime often
goes down as well, making personalist dictatorships less long-
lived than dominant-party dictatorships.

What Other Factors Influence the Chance
an Authoritarian Regime Will Fall?

There are a variety of factors that put dictatorships at risk
of collapse, ranging from an unexpected event, such as the

self-immolation of Mohamed Bouazizi in the rural town of Sidi Boudiz in 2010 that sparked the protests that took down the Tunisian dictatorship the following year, to poor decision-making, such as the Argentine military dictatorship's decision to invade the Falkland Islands in 1982, triggering a war with the United Kingdom that far outmatched it militarily. The list of factors that destabilize authoritarian regimes is long.[15]

That said, there are a handful of things that—generally speaking—exert a strong influence on the chance of authoritarian regime collapse. In technical terms, these are the factors that any empirical model of authoritarian regime survival would need to account for. Beyond authoritarian regime type, they include: economic development, economic growth, natural resource wealth, protest, and conflict (both civil and interstate). The first three factors increase authoritarian regime stability, while the last two decrease it.

Low economic development is strongly associated with more unstable authoritarian regimes (as well as more unstable democracies).[16] Richer dictatorships are better able to keep their citizens and elite supporters happy, thereby staving off pressures for their overthrow. This helps to explain the durability of those authoritarian regimes that are wealthy, such as Singapore under the People's Action Party and the Sultanate of Oman, and the fragility of those that are poor, as exemplified by the series of dictatorships that governed Benin from its independence in 1960 until democratization in 1991.

Poor economic growth also increases authoritarian regime instability. While economic booms help authoritarian regimes survive, economic busts put them at risk of overthrow.[17] The logic behind these dynamics is fairly simple. When times are good, ordinary citizens have fewer reasons to try to subvert a dictatorship, and elites fewer incentives to defect. During times of economic crisis, however, their calculations change. If ordinary citizens can no longer put food on the table, they can quickly become highly motivated to hit the streets in protest and seek the regime's ouster. This, in turn, can incentivize elite defections from the regime, particularly if elites themselves are seeing reductions in their own spoils of office. For these reasons, there are countless examples of economic crises precipitating the downfall of dictatorships, such as in the Soviet Union and Suharto's Indonesia.

The experience of Mexico under the Institutional Revolutionary Party (PRI) illustrates this well. After solid economic performance for a number of decades, dubbed the "Mexican Miracle," the good times came to an end by the mid-1970s. In 1982, the government defaulted on its debt, leading to a spiraling economic downturn. Over time, diminishing resources weakened the PRI's ability to distribute patronage and mobilized the opposition, ultimately leading to the party's defeat in 2000.[18] Economic prosperity bolstered the regime, while economic crisis undermined it.

Natural resource wealth is another factor that helps explain authoritarian stability. Like economic development, higher levels of natural resource wealth (as in income from resources such as oil, natural gas, and minerals) are tied to more durable authoritarian regimes.[19] Natural resource wealth boosts authoritarian survival by making it easier for regimes to distribute valuable benefits to citizens (e.g., low-priced fuel) and elites (e.g., lucrative government contracts). It also enables them to devote greater resources to the coercive apparatus, which reduces the chance of discontent within the military and elsewhere. Dictatorships rich in natural resources can essentially "buy" cooperation with the regime on behalf of key political actors. This helps to explain the remarkable stability of authoritarian regimes in the resource-rich Middle East, such as Qatar, Kuwait, Saudi Arabia, and Bahrain.

Protests, by contrast, are a destabilizing force in authoritarian regimes. Though small-scale protests are common in dictatorships, their escalation into a large mass movement can increase the chance of regime failure substantially. This is probably unsurprising given that if citizens take to the streets in large numbers to voice their anger with the regime, it is a clear sign of serious troubles. The evidence suggests that non-violent protests are particularly destabilizing for authoritarian regimes, but even violent protests elevate the risk of regime collapse.[20] Not all protests, of course, bring about regime change. Examples of authoritarian regime survival in the face of mass mobilization are many, including in Iran in 2009 following its disputed presidential election and Morocco in 2011 during the Arab Spring. Though protests by no means spell the collapse of an authoritarian regime, they do increase the baseline risk it will happen.

Finally, conflict increases the likelihood of authoritarian regime failure, whether civil or interstate in nature. In any given year, a fifth of all dictatorships are in the midst of some form of conflict. Given the pervasiveness of conflict in the authoritarian world, its onset does not signal that authoritarian regime collapse is imminent. At the same time, when authoritarian regimes are on the losing side of conflicts, they are at a heightened risk of falling from power. Reflecting this, 12 percent of dictatorships exit via insurgency or a foreign power's imposition, as discussed at the start of this chapter. Though there are protracted conflicts that regimes are able to endure, such as the Assad regime's ability to remain in power in Syria (as of 2017) despite a devastating civil war that has persisted since 2011, there are also plenty of examples of regime collapse in the face of conflict, such as Amin's overthrow in 1979 following Uganda's defeat in its war with Tanzania. Conflicts escalate the risk of authoritarian regime breakdown because when regimes lose them, they are often forced out afterward.

There are countless other factors that can affect the chance that an authoritarian regime will fall from power, but authoritarian regime type, economic development, economic growth, natural resource wealth, protest, and conflict are some of the more common and influential factors across cases.

What Happens after Authoritarian Regimes Fall?

When authoritarian regimes fall, there are three broad potential outcomes.[21] The first is a transition to a new authoritarian regime, such as in Armenia in 1998 when the dictatorship of Levon Ter-Petrosyan was ousted, only to be replaced by the dictatorship of Robert Kocharyan. The second outcome is that they transition to democracy, such as what occurred in Kyrgyzstan in 2010 when the regime of Kurmanbek Bakiyev was forced out of power because of a mass uprising that quickly spread across the country protesting government corruption and economic mismanagement; democratic elections were held not long thereafter. And the third outcome is that they transition to a failed state or the state ceases to exist altogether, as happened following the collapse of Barre's regime in Somalia in 1991 or Communist rule in the Soviet Union that same year.

From 1946 to 2014, new authoritarian regimes succeeded those that fell about half of the time, democracies did about the other half of the time, and only rarely did the state itself collapse.[22] This means that the end of an authoritarian regime may bring democracy afterward, but it very well may not.

In the post–Cold War period, this is less so, given the dramatic rise in democratizations we have witnessed. Since 1990, 70 percent of all authoritarian regimes democratized after leaving power, a sizable increase.[23] Even so, these statistics still reveal that 30 percent of authoritarian regimes that fall from power transition to a new authoritarian regime or give way to the dissolution of the state.

Why Is It Important to Understand That Democratization Is Not the Only Outcome?

Sometimes authoritarian regimes collapse and democracy comes next, but other times they fall and a new authoritarian regime emerges instead or, even worse, no regime at all. This is important to emphasize for two reasons.

First, if we are interested in understanding the factors that influence authoritarian regime failure broadly speaking, but identify democratization as the only end result, this can lead to misleading conclusions. Analyses of authoritarian regime failure that solely look at democratization will be unable to recognize those factors that affect transitions to new dictatorship but not transitions to democracy. For example, research shows that violent protests increase the chance of authoritarian regime collapse because they raise the risk that a dictatorship will transition to a new dictatorship.[24] Violent protests do not, however, affect the chance of democratization, specifically. If we just look at the effect of violent protests on democratic transitions, we will see little relationship and erroneously conclude that such events do not destabilize authoritarian regimes.

Second, if we are interested in identifying the factors that shape democratization but assume that all authoritarian regimes end in democracy, we run into the opposite problem. We risk conflating those things that influence transitions to new dictatorship with those that influence transitions to democracy. They may in some instances affect both, but—as the protest example illustrates—we cannot assume so. The policy implications here are fairly obvious. Foreign pressures may hasten the downfall of a notorious authoritarian regime, but a democratic successor is by no means assured.

What Is Democratization?

Democratization is the process of transitioning from some other political system type—nearly always dictatorship—to one that is democratic in nature. Determining when democratization occurs, therefore, requires an operating definition of what makes a country democratic.

There are a multitude of ways of defining democracy, but the definition used here—and in the bulk of the research referenced in this chapter—is procedural. In this sense, democracy is a political system in which citizens select their government in electoral contests that are free and fair.[25] Holding elections is a necessary component of democratic rule, but not a sufficient one. After all, most countries in the world hold regular elections. To qualify as a democracy, electoral contests must be both free and fair, such that most adult citizens are able to vote, there is real competition for the most important political posts, and citizens are truly presented a choice in terms of who will represent them, among other criteria.

Some definitions of democracy incorporate not only electoral competitiveness, but also whether the government represents the interests of the citizenry and is accountable to them. Certainly, many agree that representation and accountability are desirable from a normative perspective, but they do not guarantee democracy. Many authoritarian regimes are able to perform well in these areas, without actually giving their citizens any real say in *who* will represent them. This is a problem that procedural definitions are able to avert.

Most data sets that measure democracy cross-nationally use some form of procedural definition and, as a result, are highly correlated (at about 85 percent on average).[26] There are, of course, occasional instances of sizable expert disagreement. Botswana is a notable example. This book, like a number of others, classifies Botswana as authoritarian since independence in 1966; other studies, however, consider it democratic throughout this same time frame! In this case, the dispute centers on whether elections in Botswana truly give opponents an equal playing field, in light of the absence of public funding for opposition political parties, their limited access to the media, and features of the electoral system that advantage the incumbent Botswana Democratic Party.[27] Elections may be free in Botswana, but it is debated whether they are fair. In most data sets, however, large disparities in the classification of democracies such as this are for the most part infrequent.

Measuring a transition to democracy specifically, however, can be trickier. On the one hand, a transition to democracy is not complete unless it involves a free and fair election. The method through which the outgoing regime collapsed may not be electoral (such as a coup or popular uprising), but at some point afterward a democratic election must occur. This should make it fairly simple to assess whether a country has democratized, particularly given the pervasiveness of international election monitoring groups in the post–Cold War era that issue statements regarding the freeness and fairness of electoral contests. On the other hand, however, disagreements can emerge when identifying the precise timing of a democratic transition. For example, some observers classify the democratization date in Chile as 1989, when Patricio Aylwin won the presidential election. Yet others see it as occurring in 1990, when General Agosto Pinochet actually stepped down. Though such differences are usually minor (with one data set seeing a transition one year, and another one seeing it the next), they can result in low correlations across data sets in the identification of democratic transitions and, consequently, lead to contradictory results in studies within the democratization literature.[28]

Is Democratization the Same as Political Liberalization?

The terms "democratization" and "political liberalization" are often used interchangeably, but they refer to distinct processes.[29] Political liberalization is defined as "any change in a political system that makes that politics of that system more participatory and/or competitive."[30] Such changes can occur as part of a transition to democracy, but they often do not. For example, we frequently see political liberalization in well-established authoritarian regimes, such as when Mobutu introduced multiparty electoral competition in the Democratic Republic of Congo (then Zaire) in 1990, but continued to govern in virtually the same fashion until his ouster in 1997. We also see political liberalization in longtime democracies, such as when the United States extended suffrage to 18- to 20-year-old citizens via a 1971 amendment to its constitution. Political liberalization can occur in a variety of political contexts, only some of which are manifestations of transition to democracy. Democratization implies political liberalization, but political liberalization may or may not imply democratization.

Why Is It Dangerous to Conflate the Two?

It is dangerous to conflate democratization and political liberalization because many reforms often considered to be signs of political liberalization are actually associated with greater authoritarian regime survival. As discussed elsewhere in this book, many authoritarian regimes adopt the same institutions that we have historically viewed as quintessential hallmarks of democracies—including elections, parties, and legislatures—even though they have no intention of using them for democratic purposes. These and other pseudo-democratic institutions may make it easier for opposition groups to organize, operate, and mobilize, but at the expense of helping the authoritarian regime more effectively deal with threats to its rule. There is quite a bit of evidence, for example, that multiparty elections are occasions for authoritarian regimes to learn about the preferences of rival politicians and the citizenry, information that they leverage to help prolong their time in office.[31]

This is not to say that political liberalization brings no benefits to those who oppose the regime. For many, it is likely preferable to challenge the regime in a political environment that is more participatory and competitive than in one that is less so. Citizens may even see such gains as worth it, even if they stave off democratization.

It is also true that, occasionally, reforms that constitute political liberalization but fall short of a transition to democracy do indeed reflect a genuine effort to democratize. For example, we know that in Bhutan the ruling monarchy actually intended to step down from power at some point in the years to come and transition the country to democracy when it held Bhutan's first subnational election in 2002.[32] Without the benefit of hindsight, however, it is difficult to sort out the true meaning of such actions. Observers were quick to view the 2015 elections in Myanmar, for example, as a sign of democratization following decades of military rule. Yet, multiple developments since—such as the military's escalation of its ethnic cleansing campaign against the Rohingya—suggest that it remains politically powerful, prompting many to change their tune.[33]

For these reasons, we should pause before assuming that political liberalization in authoritarian regimes suggests an increase in the democratic nature of the regimes governing them. Rather than signaling an impending democratic transition, political liberalization may instead work to forestall it.

Do Pseudo-Democratic Institutions Affect the Chance of Democratization?

Today's authoritarian regimes are particularly fond of incorporating institutions that seem democratic—such as political parties, elections, and legislatures. Most experts see this as an intentional part of their survival strategy, rather than a reflection of any serious attempt to democratize, as covered earlier in this chapter. And, indeed, the evidence shows that authoritarian regimes that feature pseudo-democratic institutions last longer in power than those that do not.[34]

While dictatorships with seemingly democratic institutions are more durable than their institution-free counterparts are, there is evidence that when they do collapse, they are more likely to democratize.[35] This means that though pseudo-democratic institutions help authoritarian regimes hold on to power, they also put them on a better path toward democratizing in the long run.

As real-world examples, consider the cases of Mexico under the PRI and Taiwan under the Kuomintang. In both instances, the regime mimicked democratic rule by holding regular

elections and allowing opposition parties to have representation in the legislature. Both regimes were also remarkably
long-lived: the PRI governed Mexico from 1915 to 2000 and
the Kuomintang governed Taiwan from 1949 to 2000. In both
cases, the regime collapsed and democracy succeeded it.

Do Features of the Transition Affect the Chance of Democratization?

Characteristics of an authoritarian regime's transition out of
power are influential in determining what happens next.[36] For
one, when authoritarian regimes are forced out of power, as
opposed to when they leave it on their own terms, the chance
of democratization is quite a bit lower. In the period 1946 to
2014, forced overthrows (which include foreign impositions,
coups, popular uprisings, and insurgencies) only led to democratization in about 1 in 5 cases; departures that did not
occur through overt force (which include elections and rule
changes that alter the composition of the ruling elite), by contrast, did so about three-quarters of the time.

Similarly, whether there is violence at the time of the transition is an important predictor of whether democracy will result. Nonviolent transitions see democratization follow them
54 percent of the time, compared to 40 percent of transitions
that are violent.

These basic statistics suggest that violent, forceful authoritarian regime transitions are far less likely to lead to democratization than those that are not.

Does Authoritarian Regime Type Affect the Chance of Democratization?

Authoritarian regime type helps explain differences in the
vulnerabilities of dictatorships to collapse. It also helps explain differences in their chances of democratizing. Military
dictatorships are the most likely regime type to transition to

democratize, personalist dictatorships are the least likely, and dominant-party dictatorships are somewhere in between. Figure 8.3 illustrates these patterns. It shows that 64 percent of military dictatorships democratize after falling from power, compared to 38 percent of dominant-party dictatorships and 36 percent of personalist dictatorships.

There are two dynamics that help explain these differences, which draw from insights discussed earlier in this chapter.[37] First, military dictatorships are more likely than other forms of authoritarianism to negotiate their own transitions out of office. Such non-coerced exits are particularly amenable to democratization. Examples that illustrate this include the Chilean military dictatorship's departure from office in 1989, which took place following a referendum vote that the regime lost on whether it should continue to govern, and the Brazilian military dictatorship's decision to step down in 1985 after its favored candidate lost an electoral college vote for the presidency. In both instances, democratization followed the transition.

Second, personalist dictatorships are the most likely of all authoritarian regimes to cling to power until the very end

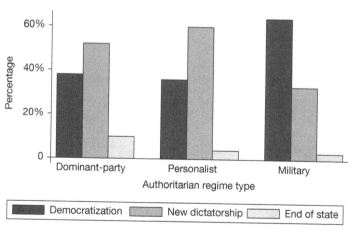

Figure 8.3 What happens after authoritarian regimes fall, by type: 1946 to 2010.

because they are likely to encounter negative repercussions should they leave it, such as imprisonment, exile, or death. They often have to be forced out of office as a result, and their exits are frequently violent. Such conditions bode poorly for democratization. There are many examples of this occurring, such as Muammar Gaddafi's bloody ouster in Libya during that country's civil war in 2011 and Fulgencio Batista's overthrow at the hands of Communist insurgents in Cuba in 1959. In neither instance did democracy emerge afterward.

Do Coups Affect the Chance of Democratization?

When military officers seize power in a coup, they often issue statements asserting that they promise to transition the country to democracy soon afterward. After the 2015 coup in Burkina Faso that toppled strongman Blaise Compaore, for example, the military announced, "We are not here to stay in power. As soon as conditions are there we will hand power back to [civilians]."[38] In some cases, military officers fulfill such promises, as in the case of Burkina Faso where free and fair elections were held later that year. Such experiences have prompted some observers to see coups as an opportunity for democratization, arguing that "coups and the threat of coups can be a significant weapon in fostering democracy."[39]

It is true that coups in authoritarian regimes raise the baseline risk of democratization in a given year, by creating openings for political reform that otherwise would not exist. So-called democratization coups have occurred in a number of places, such as in Niger in 2010, when the military took control of the presidential palace and detained then-President Mamadou Tandja. Military officers subsequently established the Supreme Council for the Restoration of Democracy, which oversaw democratic elections the following year. Democratization coups have also occurred in Portugal in 1974, Mali in 1991, and Guinea Bissau in 2003, to name but a few examples.

Though coups in authoritarian regimes generate opportunities for political change that in some instances result in democratization, more often than not they simply lead to a leadership change or the installation of a new authoritarian regime.[40] The evidence indicates that coup plotters typically overthrow authoritarian leaders just to replace them with new ones or with new regimes altogether. This is indeed what has occurred in a majority of cases, including Guinea in 2008, Cote d'Ivoire in 1999, and Niger in 1996.

To summarize, while coups increase a dictatorship's baseline chance of democratizing, they increase the chance of a new authoritarian regime emerging even more so.

Does Natural Resource Wealth Affect the Chance of Democratization?

Observers have noted for some time a link between natural resource wealth and authoritarian durability (one branch of the so-called resource curse literature).[41] Examples include Russia, Saudi Arabia, Iran, and Angola. Though the resource curse literature suggests that natural resource wealth prolongs authoritarianism by reducing pressures for democracy, the recent research finds little evidence of this.[42] Rather, natural resource–rich dictatorships are long-lasting because they can use their resource income to purchase the support of key political actors and beef up the security sector, lessening the likelihood that rival authoritarian groups will try to seek their overthrow. In other words, natural resource wealth boosts regime survival not by decreasing prospects for democratization, but by lowering the chance of transition to a new authoritarian regime.[43]

One of the central messages, therefore, is that natural resource wealth helps authoritarian regimes endure. This does not necessarily mean that it is a curse for the citizens living in such countries, however. While it is possible that they would fare better under a democracy, it is also possible that they would fare worse in a country in which one authoritarian regime succeeds another over and over again. As an example of this, consider the different political realities citizens face in Yemen, a natural resource–poor country that has experienced a series of distinct authoritarian governments over the past few decades that often emerged via bloody and violent transitions, with those they face in neighboring Saudi Arabia, a natural resource–rich country governed by a single authoritarian monarchy since its independence.

Do Sanctions Affect the Chance of Democratization?

The goals of most economic sanctions levied against authoritarian regimes is to sap their leadership groups of the resources they need to maintain control and keep their supporters contented. Many observers, however, question whether sanctions work, citing examples such as the U.S. embargo of Cuba, which did little to destabilize the Castro dictatorship but may very well be hurting ordinary Cubans; or the prolonged international sanctions on North Korea in response to its nuclear ambitions, which do not seem to have affected the Kim family's rule, though they have surely exacted a heavy toll on the North Korean economy.[44]

Whether sanctions are an effective foreign policy tool is an important question, given that it is one increasingly used. Between 1914 and 1945, there were just 12 cases of sanctions, a number that increased to more than 50 in the 1990s.[45]

Research looking at the impact of sanctions on authoritarian *leader* survival suggests that sometimes sanctions destabilize dictators but other times they do not. The effectiveness of sanctions is dependent on the regime type of the target. Specifically, sanctions are most likely to increase leadership vulnerabilities when used against personalist dictatorships than against other forms of authoritarianism.[46] Leaders in personalist dictatorships are more reliant on patronage networks to maintain control, making them more sensitive than other leaders to losses of external income. When sanctions limit the resources at their disposal to pay off supporters, personalist rulers lack the institutions needed to execute an alternate strategy. They may try to ratchet up repression, but this can backfire and further threaten their rule. For this reason, sanctions can destabilize personalist leaders but are less likely to destabilize other authoritarian leaders.

This tells us little, however, about whether sanctions affect prospects for democratization, given that leadership change may or may not lead to regime change and regime change may or may not lead to democracy. The evidence in this regard overall is mixed. In some instances sanctions work to promote democracy, in others they do nothing, and in others they are counterproductive. That said, there is evidence that *democratic* sanctions, which have the specific intended goal of improving levels of democracy, increase political liberalization.[47] Political liberalization does not guarantee democratization—far from it, as covered earlier in this chapter—but it does mean greater political participation and contestation. As an example, the United States sanctioned Peru in 1992 by withdrawing military and economic assistance to the country after then-President Alberto Fujimori closed the legislature and initiated his *autogolpe*. Democratization in Peru did not occur until 2000, when a corruption scandal forced Fujimori out of power, but levels of political liberalization at least increased as Fujimori's tenure progressed.[48]

In sum, though the jury is out regarding whether sanctions actually increase the odds of an authoritarian regime transitioning to democracy, sanctions do make personalist leaders vulnerable to overthrow and those that specifically seek to promote democracy increase prospects of political liberalization.

Does Foreign Aid Affect the Chance of Democratization?

Another foreign policy tool that is often used to pressure authoritarian regimes to pursue reforms is foreign aid. Foreign donors allocate aid to a target country in hopes of incentivizing that country to implement desired policies.

Statistics show that distribution of foreign aid is on the rise. Looking just at sub-Saharan Africa, for example, foreign aid per capita increased from under $50 per person in 1997 to around $85 in 2007, with total foreign aid allotted to the region going up more than twofold.[49] Most targets of foreign aid are authoritarian regimes.

Allocation of foreign aid as a method for encouraging reforms, however, has come under substantial criticism. There are, after all, a number of famous cases of Western aid actually helping notorious dictators maintain power, as was likely true with Mobutu of former Zaire. Supporting this critique, a large body of research shows that authoritarian regimes are skillful at using foreign aid to prolong their rule.[50]

At the same time, not all authoritarian regimes are likely to squander foreign aid. The evidence suggests that some authoritarian regimes are more apt than others to use foreign aid for its intended purposes. Foreign aid given to dominant-party dictatorships, in particular, is most likely to lead to democratization. Key political actors in dominant-party dictatorships often have a reasonable shot of winning competitive elections should they step down from power. The costs of leaving office, in other words, may not be that high for them. Because they have a chance of returning to power if they liberalize, they are more likely to be swayed by pressures tied to foreign aid.[51]

Moreover, not all types of foreign aid are the same. Since the end of the Cold War, donors are increasingly allocating foreign aid for the explicit purpose of fostering democratization. In the United States alone, resources for democracy promotion programs grew a whopping 538 percent between 1990 and 2003, while total assistance only increased 19 percent.[52] Studies examining the impact of this specific form of aid reveal that it can, in fact, be effective in bringing about political liberalization.[53] Pro-democracy foreign aid increases the chance of multiparty politics and decreases incidences of electoral mis-conduct.[54] But, it is important to note, such reforms may not actually threaten authoritarian incumbents, for all the reasons discussed in this chapter.

Taken together, the evidence indicates that the effectiveness of foreign aid in encouraging democratization is very much context dependent. Foreign aid is more likely to succeed in bringing about transition to democracy when dominant-party dictatorships are the target. In addition, aid is more likely to increase political liberalization when it is explicitly directed toward strengthening political institutions and civil society. Further research is needed, however, to ascertain whether this type of aid also increases prospects for democratization specifically.

Do Nonviolent Protests Affect the Chance of Democratization?

Most protests do not lead to the downfall of authoritarian regimes, though they do increase the baseline risk of it occurring, as discussed earlier in this chapter. Importantly, when protests do topple dictatorships, they do not always pave the way for transition to democracy afterward. Evidence of protests ushering in new authoritarian regimes are many, such as the Iranian revolution that ousted the Shah but brought to power a group of theocrats in 1979, the massive demonstrations in Myanmar that triggered a coup that forced one faction of the military out of power but replaced it with a new one in 1988, and the widespread protests in Kyrgyzstan that led to then-President Askar Akayev's resignation but were followed by rigged elections that guaranteed the victory of Kurmanbek Bakiyev in 2005.

In all three of these examples, protests involved violence. This is not coincidental: violent protests increase the chance of authoritarian collapse and transition to new authoritarianism. Nonviolent protests, by contrast, raise the likelihood of a transition to democracy.[55]

The experience of the Philippines under Ferdinand Marcos helps illustrate this dynamic. After the murder of anti-Marcos politician Ninoy Aquino in 1983, the opposition joined forces to back his widow, Corazon Aquino, in the 1986 presidential race. Marcos won the contest, albeit with the help of massive electoral fraud. Huge mass protests began in response, which had the support of key actors, such as the Catholic Church and senior members of the military.[56] Corazon Aquino made clear that such activities needed to remain peaceful, telling crowds, "I'm not asking for violent revolution. This is not the time for that. I always indicated that now is the way of nonviolent struggle for justice."[57] As pressures mounted, troops loyal to Marcos refused to shoot at the crowds, and four days later Marcos was forced into exile. Corazon Aquino was installed as president soon thereafter and moved quickly to ratify a new constitution and establish a new congress, ushering in a period of democratic rule.

Though protests of all forms make authoritarian regimes vulnerable to collapse, levels of violence are important in driving whether new authoritarian regimes or democratic ones succeed those that fall.

9

CONCLUSION

What Did You Learn in This Book?

Well, hopefully, quite a lot. This book is intended to put readers on more solid footing for understanding authoritarian politics. To do so, it describes how politics works in authoritarian contexts and how this, in turn, influences outcomes we care about.

Chapter 1 introduced the book and specified its major themes. It explained why authoritarianism matters and highlighted the challenges inherent in studying authoritarian rule. It defined a number of key concepts, such as what we mean by the term "authoritarian regime," and reviewed how these conceptualizations have evolved. It also set the stage for one of the book's central themes, which is the importance of looking at trends over time in our analyses of authoritarian politics. Today's dictatorships behave in ways different from those of the past. While it is important to identify broad commonalities across the authoritarian regimes that have existed throughout history, it is also important to bring to the fore those developments and features that are unique to contemporary dictatorships.

Chapter 2 provided some basic information about authoritarian politics to guide the discussion to follow. It outlined who the key actors are in authoritarian regimes and defined their major goals. It also covered how these actors relate with one another, shedding light on the dynamic nature of authoritarian rule. It then explained the importance of differentiating authoritarian regimes from authoritarian leaders, as well as differentiating authoritarian regimes from consecutive periods of authoritarianism. Iraq, for example, has been authoritarian from its independence in 1932 until the present, a period during which it has seen six unique authoritarian and ten distinct authoritarian leaders. Conflation of these units of analysis can lead to misguided understandings of the rise and fall of both authoritarian regimes and the leaders who rule them.

Chapter 3 surveyed the authoritarian landscape. It discussed where we have seen authoritarianism emerge historically since World War II, as well as where we are most likely to see it today. All but four of today's authoritarian regimes govern in sub-Saharan African, Asia, or the Middle East and North Africa. It offered insight into these trends by explaining why authoritarianism has been more common in the developing world, as well as why and when we have seen waves of democratizations and their reverse. It also provides evidence that we are in the midst of a modest resurgence of authoritarianism after many years of decline, though this could be due to global decreases in levels of political liberalization in authoritarian regimes and democracies, as opposed to incidences of transition from democracy to dictatorship.

Chapter 4 narrowed the lens to examine authoritarian leadership. It identified the key strategies that authoritarian leaders use to maintain control and explained why some seem more powerful than others. It discussed the phenomenon of personalization, or the consolidation of power into the hands of a single individual, and—given its consequences for a number of political outcomes of interest—listed key signals that it is occurring. Chapter 4 also reviewed how authoritarian leaders leave power, how this has changed over time, and how fear of punishment after departing can influence their behaviors while still in office. Though some dictators enjoy a peaceful retirement after their exits, others are not so fortunate. Dictators who assess they are contenders for imprisonment, exile, or death after being ousted cling to power until the bitter end, even if doing so means plunging their countries into periods of violence and bloodshed.

Chapter 5 begins with the assumption that authoritarian regimes differ from one another in important ways and discusses how they can be grouped. It presents the regime typology relied on throughout this book—the disaggregation of authoritarian regimes as personalist, military, dominant-party, or monarchic—and shows how differences in type can inform our understanding of a number of key political outcomes. It also offers evidence that there have been changes in the distribution of authoritarian regime types over time such that personalist dictatorships have become increasingly common and military dictatorships less so. All signs indicate that this trend is set to continue, in light of the emergence of a number of new personalist dictatorships in the past few years, such as in Turkey in 2016 and Burundi in 2010.

The chapters that follow cover the arc of authoritarian rule, detailing how authoritarian regimes rise to power, the strategies they use to maintain it, and how they fall. Chapter 6 examines how authoritarian rulers seize control. Coups have historically been the most common method through which new authoritarian regimes have formed, but there are signs that this is changing. Authoritarianizations, in which incumbents leverage their position of power to consolidate control, have increased since the end of the Cold War and are on track to outpace coups in frequency. This chapter explains these dynamics, identifies the telltale indicators of authoritarianization, and explains how populist rhetoric can pave the way for such takeovers. Importantly, it gives evidence that authoritarianizations are increasingly ushering in personalist rule, as the aforementioned examples of Turkey and Burundi illustrate.

Chapter 7 focuses on the survival strategies of authoritarian regimes, specifically the use of repression and co-optation. It defines both of these survival tools, reviews the various ways in which authoritarian regimes employ them, and shows how their use varies across authoritarian regime types. It also documents how reliance on repression and co-optation in authoritarian regimes has evolved over time. For one, post–Cold War authoritarian regimes are increasingly moving away from blunt and overt repressive tactics and repressing in a subtler and more ambiguous fashion. They might use lawsuits to muzzle opponents, for example, rather than simply arresting them. Similarly, today's authoritarian regimes have broadened the ways in which they use co-optation. The tactics they rely on to secure the support of potential challengers and incentivize regime compliance are expanding, such as the creation of government-organized nongovernmental organizations to co-opt civil society groups. Most of these changes in the survival strategies of authoritarian regimes make contemporary regimes appear more democratic, albeit in form only. They are associated with longer-lasting authoritarianism.

Chapter 8 provides basic information on how authoritarian regimes leave power. Coups were traditionally the most frequent mode of collapse, but since the Cold War's end they have been displaced by elections. Popular uprisings have also become more common, accounting for a fifth of today's authoritarian regime failures. This chapter additionally surveys the key factors that increase the likelihood authoritarian regimes will fall from power, including authoritarian regime type and economic conditions, emphasizing that about half of authoritarian regimes leave power only to be replaced by new ones. Democratic rule following collapse, in other words, is far from guaranteed. It then focuses on democratization specifically. It explains what democratization is and the factors that influence it, stressing the criticality of differentiating democratization from political liberalization more generally. There are many things that we know can cause authoritarian regimes to become more participatory and open to political competition; we cannot assume, however, that these same factors also cause them to be more likely to democratize.

What Lies Ahead in the Field of Authoritarianism?

A number of critical unanswered questions remain in terms of our understanding of authoritarian politics. First, we know that personalist rule is not only on the rise, but also that it is associated with a range of bad outcomes. Personalist dictators start more wars, behave in unpredictable yet belligerent ways, are more likely to steal from state coffers, and are unlikely to democratize, to name just a few negative repercussions of this form of authoritarianism. We know less, however, about the conditions that lead to strongman rule, as opposed to more collegial types of dictatorship. Seizure groups that are more fractured and less institutionalized facilitate the emergence of a one-man dictatorship after the seizure occurs, but what are the factors associated with these types of groups gaining control in the first place versus those that are better structured and organized?[1]

Second, authoritarianizations are emerging as one of the most common ways that democracies fall apart and new dictatorships emerge. With authoritarianizations, incumbents slowly chip away at the political institutions of the democracies they were freely and fairly elected in. The end result of this process is the establishment of authoritarian rule. Such takeovers are difficult for opposition groups to mobilize against, due to their incremental and ambiguous nature. They are also increasingly likely to give rise to personalist dictatorship. Better understanding the conditions that enable authoritarianizations is therefore of particular importance. There is some evidence that natural resource wealth and presidentialism increase the chance of an incumbent takeover, but more research is needed to further explore these dynamics and identify additional factors that matter.[2] Gaining insight into these issues would not only fill a gap in the academic literature on authoritarianism, but also inform the strategies opposition groups and democracy advocates pursue to counteract incumbent efforts to dismantle the democracies they rule.

Third, today's dictatorships have evolved in considerable ways over the past few decades. More now than ever, they adopt features of democracy, albeit in name only, as a method for maintaining their rule. Most evidence suggests that they are wise to do so. Authoritarian regimes that feature pseudo-democratic institutions, for example, last longer in power than those that do not. Though they are more likely to democratize when they do transition out of power, such transitions are often a long time coming. This means that political liberalization, in the form of greater contestation and participation, which often comes with the adoption of institutions such as political parties, elections, and legislatures, may actually reflect a savvy authoritarian government rather than a real effort for political reform. It is therefore very difficult to disentangle the meaning of political liberalization in authoritarian regimes. Under what conditions does it signal that democracy is on the horizon? Are there specific manifestations of political liberalization that are more likely to encourage democratization than others? While we can never get into the minds of dictators to understand their true intentions, we may be able to examine whether certain components of political liberalization increase the odds of democratization in the nearer term.

Fourth, some authoritarian regimes democratize only to collapse to renewed dictatorship not long afterward. Think of Egypt's short-lived experience with democracy under President Mohamed Morsi, which began following the 2012 elections that brought him to power and ended with the military coup that unseated him the following year. Despite sentiments that democracy was long overdue in Egypt—Morsi was the first Egyptian leader ever elected freely and fairly there—such aspirations were quickly dashed. Democratic experiences have been brief in plenty of other countries as well, such as Azerbaijan from 1992 to 1993, Burundi from 1993 to 1996 and again from 2005 to 2010, and Republic of Congo from 1992 to 1997. Better understanding democratic consolidation— the process through which a newly established democracy becomes one that is durable—is therefore important. Though we know some things about the conditions that favor democratic consolidation,[3] we know substantially less about how features of the outgoing authoritarian regime do. Most studies in the field of authoritarianism examine the factors that increase the chance of democratic transitions but do not assess whether they also increase the prospects that such transitions will lead to long-lasting democracy. Gaining insight into these issues would be valuable and pave the way for more informed strategies for new democracies to protect themselves from renewed authoritarianism.

These are but a few of the unanswered questions in the field of authoritarianism. There are surely others. Gaining ground on these, however, would fill a number of timely and critical gaps.

This book closes with a reminder that authoritarian regimes do not appear to be disappearing any time soon. Around 40 percent of the world's people live under some form of authoritarian rule today, with the Chinese Communist regime alone governing about a fifth of them. By modest estimates, authoritarian regimes rule about a third of the world's countries. Though this marks a drop from the Cold War era, there are few indications that they will continue to decrease in number. Improving our understanding of how politics works within them therefore remains as important a task as ever.

NOTES

Chapter 1

1   Ella Morton, "Golden Statues and Mother Bread: The Bizarre Legacy of Turkmenistan's Former Dictator," *Slate*, February 6, 2014, http://www.slate.com/blogs/atlas_obscura/2014/02/06/saparmurat_niyazov_former_president_of_turkmenistan_has_left_quite_the_legacy.html, accessed October 2, 2017; "Factbox: Gaddafi Rule Marked by Abuses, Rights Groups Say," *Reuters*, February 22, 2011, https://www.reuters.com/article/us-libya-protest-abuses/factbox-gaddafi-rule-marked-by-abuses-rights-groups-say-idUSTRE71L1NH20110222, accessed October 2, 2017.

2   Natina Tan, "Institutionalized Hegemonic Party Rule in Singapore," in *Party Institutionalization in Asia: Democracies, Autocracies and the Shadows of the Past*, edited by Erik Kuhonta and Allen Hicken (New York, NY: Cambridge University Press, 2015), pp. 49–73.

3   "Freedom in the World 2017," Freedom House, https://freedomhouse.org/report/freedom-world/freedom-world-2017, accessed October 2, 2017.

4   These statistics come from the Autocratic Regimes Data Set and my own updates to this data set. See Barbara Geddes, Joseph Wright, and Erica Frantz, "Autocratic Breakdown and Regime Transitions: A New Data Set," *Perspectives on Politics* 12, no. 2 (2014): pp. 313–331.

5   Jeffrey Conroy-Krutz and Erica Frantz, "Theories of Democratic Change Phase II: Paths Away from Authoritarianism," USAID,

September 1, 2017, https://www.iie.org/Research-and-Insights/ Publications.

6 Stanley G. Payne, "Twentieth-Century Dictatorships: The Ideological One-Party States," *American Historical Review* 101, no. 4 (1996): p. 1187.

7 Oisin Tansey, *The International Politics of Authoritarian Rule* (Oxford, UK: Oxford University Press, 2016), p. 3.

8 Martin Stuart Fox, "Laos: Politics in a Single-Party State," *Southeast Asian Affairs* (2007): pp. 159–180.

9 "Laos Country Profile," *BBC News*, June 14, 2017, http://www. bbc.com/news/world-asia-pacific-15351898, accessed October 2, 2017.

10 "Laos Comes Up Short Again on Annual International Press Freedom Ranking," Radio Free Asia, April 20, 2016, http:// www.rfa.org/english/news/laos/laos-comes-up-short-again-on-annual-international-press-freedom-ranking-04202016161328. html, accessed October 2, 2017.

11 Sheila Fitzpatrick, *On Stalin's Team: The Years of Living Dangerously in Soviet Politics* (Princeton, NJ: Princeton University Press, 2015), p. 278.

12 "Medvedev Insists He's the Boss in Russia," *Reuters,* March 29, 2009, http://www.reuters.com/article/us-russia-medvedev-power/medvedev-insists-hes-the-boss-in-russia-idUSTRE52S0W720090329, accessed October 13, 2017.

13 Christopher S. P. Magee, and John A. Doces, "Reconsidering Regime Type and Growth: Lies, Dictatorships, and Statistics," *International Studies Quarterly* 59, no. 2 (2014): pp. 223–237.

14 Paul H. Lewis, "Salazar's Ministerial Elite, 1932–1968," *Journal of Politics* 40, no. 3 (1978): p. 622.

15 Geddes, Wright, and Frantz, "Autocratic Breakdown and Regime Transitions," p. 327.

16 Ibid., p. 317.

17 Philippe C. Schmitter and Terry Lynn Karl, "What Democracy Is . . . and Is Not," *Journal of Democracy* 2, no. 3 (1991): pp. 75–88.

18 Adam Przeworski, Michael Alvarez, Jose Antonio Cheibub, and Fernando Limongi, *Democracy and Development: Political Institutions and Well-Being in the World, 1950–1990* (Cambridge, UK: Cambridge University Press, 2000), pp. 15–18.

19 Regime start and end data used in this book come from Geddes, Wright, and Frantz, "Autocratic Breakdown and Regime Transitions."

20 Paul Brooker, *Non-Democratic Regimes: Theory, Government, and Politics* (London, UK: Macmillan Press, 2000).

21 Jeffrey C. Isaac, *Democracy in Dark Times* (Ithaca, NY: Cornell University Press, 1998), p. 26.

22 Erica Frantz, "Autocracy," in *Oxford Research Encyclopedia of Politics* (2016), http://politics.oxfordre.com/view/10.1093/acrefore/9780190228637.001.0001/acrefore-9780190228637-e-3, accessed October 2, 2017.

23 Carl Schmitt, *Dictatorship* (Cambridge, UK: Polity Press, [1921] 2013).

24 Emilio Rabasa, *La Constitución y la Dictadura. Estudio Sobre la Organización Política de México* (Mexico City, Mexico: Porrúa, [1912] 1976).

25 Hannah Arendt, *The Origins of Totalitarianism* (New York, NY: Schocken Books, 1951), p. 323.

26 Frantz, "Autocracy."

27 Richard Snyder and James Mahoney, "The Missing Variable: Institutions and the Study of Regime Change," *Comparative Politics* 32, no. 1 (1999): pp. 103–122.

28 Samuel P. Huntington and Clement H. Moore, *Authoritarian Politics in Modern Society: The Dynamics of Established One-Party Systems* (New York, NY: Basic Books, 1970).

29 Amos Perlmutter, *The Military and Politics in Modern Times* (New Haven, CT: Yale University Press, 1977).

30 Michael Bratton and Nicolas Van de Walle, *Democratic Experiments in Africa: Regime Transitions in Comparative Perspective* (Cambridge, UK: Cambridge University Press, 1997).

31 Ibid.

32 Jennifer Gandhi and Ellen Lust-Okar, "Elections Under Authoritarianism," *Annual Review of Political Science* 12 (2009): pp. 403–422.

33 Andrea Kendall-Taylor and Erica Frantz, "Mimicking Democracy to Prolong Autocracies," *Washington Quarterly* 37, no. 4 (2014): pp. 71–84.

34 Ibid.

35 Geddes, Wright, and Frantz, "Autocratic Breakdown and Regime Transitions."

Chapter 2

1 This subset of the population is akin to the concept of the selectorate in the selectorate theory. See Bruce Bueno de

Mesquita, Alastair Smith, Randolph M. Siverson, and James
D. Morrow, *The Logic of Political Survival* (Cambridge, MA: MIT
Press, 2003).

2 See, for example, "Is Iran's Presidential Election Free and Fair?"
RadioFreeEurope/RadioLiberty, May 1, 2017, https://www.rferl.
org/a/is-irans-presidential-election-free-and-fair/28457503.html,
accessed October 13, 2017.

3 Muhammad Sahimi, "Analysis: Ahmadinejad-Khamenei Rift
Deepens into Abyss," *Frontline PBS,* May 7, 2011, http://www.
pbs.org/wgbh/pages/frontline/tehranbureau/2011/05/
opinion-ahmadinejad-khamenei-rift-deepens-to-an-abyss.html,
accessed October 13, 2017.

4 Gordon Tullock, *Autocracy* (Boston, MA: Kluwer, 1987).

5 Geddes, Wright, and Frantz, "Autocratic Breakdown and Regime
Transitions," p. 327.

6 Ibid., p. 320.

7 "Hissene Habre: Chad's Ex-ruler Convicted of Crimes against
Humanity," *BBC News,* May 30, 2016, http://www.bbc.com/
news/world-africa-36411466, accessed October 12, 2017.

8 "Human Development Report 2016: Congo (Democratic Republic
of the)," United Nations Development Programme, 2016, http://
hdr.undp.org/sites/all/themes/hdr_theme/country-notes/
COD.pdf, accessed October 12, 2017.

9 The Torrijos regime is considered distinct from the Noriega
regime because in the former an alliance of National Guard
officers and civilians determined policy, whereas in the latter
only a faction of the National Guard and a much smaller group
of civilians did. See Barbara Geddes, Joseph Wright, and Erica
Frantz, "Autocratic Regimes Code Book," Version 1.2, *Autocratic
Regime Data,* 2014, http://sites.psu.edu/dictators/wp-content/
uploads/sites/12570/2016/05/GWF-Codebook.pdf, accessed
October 12, 2017.

10 Robert Jackson Alexander and Eldon M. Parker, *A History
of Organized Labor in Panama and Central America* (Westport,
CT: Praeger, 2008), p. 9.

11 Peter Eisner, "Manuel Noriega, Panamanian Strongman Toppled
in U.S. Invasion, Dies at 83," *The Washington Post,* May 30, 2017,
https://www.washingtonpost.com/world/the_americas/
manuel-noriega-panamanian-strongman-toppled-in-us-invasion-
dies-at-83/2017/05/30/9c2d77bc-0384-11e7-b9fa-ed727b644a0b_
story.html?utm_term=.5ed3bc0fc33a, accessed October 12, 2017.

Chapter 3

1 Barbara Geddes, "What Causes Democratization," in *The Oxford Handbook of Comparative Politics,* edited by Carles Boix and Susan Carol Stokes (Oxford, UK: Oxford University Press, 2007), pp. 317–339.

2 Ibid., p. 317.

3 Level of development is measured using GDP per capita, provided by Kristian Skrede Gleditsch, "Expanded Trade and GDP Data," *Journal of Conflict Resolution* 46, no. 5 (2002): pp. 712–724. Political system type is measured using combined Polity scores, provided by "Polity IV Project: Political Regime Characteristics and Transitions, 1800–2015," Polity IV, http://www.systemicpeace.org/polity/polity4.htm, accessed March 15, 2017. These scores range from –10 to 10, with higher scores indicating greater levels of "democraticness." Countries are considered democratic here if their scores are 7 or greater.

4 Kristian Skrede Gleditsch and Michael D. Ward, "Diffusion and the International Context of Democratization," *International Organization* 60, no. 3 (2006): pp. 911–933.

5 Carles Boix and Susan Carol Stokes, "Introduction," in *The Oxford Handbook of Comparative Politics,* edited by Carles Boix and Susan Carol Stokes (Oxford, UK: Oxford University Press, 2007), p. xiii.

6 Natasha Ezrow, Erica Frantz, and Andrea Kendall-Taylor, *Development and the State in the 21st Century: Tackling the Challenges of the Developing World* (London, UK: Palgrave Macmillan, 2015).

7 Seymour Martin Lipset, "Some Social Requisites of Democracy: Economic Development and Political Legitimacy," *American Political Science Review* 53, no. 1 (1959): pp. 69–105.

8 Barrington Moore, *Social Origins of Dictatorship and Democracy: Lord and Peasant in the Making of the Modern World* (London, UK: Penguin, 1967).

9 Ezrow, Frantz, and Kendall-Taylor, *Development and the State in the 21st Century.*

10 Christian Davenport and David A. Armstrong II, "Democracy and the Violation of Human Rights: A Statistical Analysis from 1976 to 1996," *American Journal of Political Science* 48, no. 3 (2004): pp. 538–554.

11 Robert T. Deacon, "Public Good Provision Under Dictatorship and Democracy," *Public Choice* 139, no. 1 (2009): pp. 241–262.

12 Stephen Knack and Philip Keefer, "Institutions and Economic Performance: Cross-Country Tests Using Alternative Institutional Measures," *Economics & Politics* 7, no. 3 (1995): pp. 207–227.

13 Pak Hung Mo, "Corruption and Economic Growth," *Journal of Comparative Economics* 29, no. 1 (2001): pp. 66–79; Daniel Lederman, Norman V. Loayza, and Rodrigo R. Soares, "Accountability and Corruption: Political Institutions Matter," *Economics & Politics* 17, no. 1 (2005): pp. 1–35.

14 Przeworski, Alvarez, Cheibub, and Limongi, *Democracy and Development*.

15 Geddes, "What Causes Democratization."

16 Joshua Massarenti, "Przeworski: 'No Democracy without free, competitive elections,'" *Afronline*, April 12, 2011, https://www.afronline.org/?p=14539, accessed October 26, 2017.

17 Samuel P. Huntington, "Democracy's Third Wave," *Journal of Democracy* 2, no. 2 (1991): pp. 12–34.

18 Ibid.

19 Larry Diamond, "A Fourth Wave or False Start?" *Foreign Affairs*, May 22, 2011, https://www.foreignaffairs.com/articles/middle-east/2011-05-22/fourth-wave-or-false-start, accessed October 19, 2017.

20 Huntington, "Democracy's Third Wave."

21 Ibid., p. 12.

22 Ibid., pp. 17–18.

23 "Democracy in the Former Soviet Union: 1991–2004," *Eurasianet. org*, January 2, 2005, http://www.eurasianet.org/departments/insight/articles/pp010305.shtml, accessed October 19, 2017.

24 Larry Diamond, "Is Pakistan the (Reverse) Wave of the Future?," *Journal of Democracy* 11, no. 3 (2000): pp. 91–106.

25 Andrea Kendall-Taylor and Erica Frantz, "Mimicking Democracy to Prolong Autocracies," *Washington Quarterly* 37, no. 4 (2014): pp. 71–84.

26 "Freedom in the World 2017," Freedom House, https://freedomhouse.org/report/freedom-world/freedom-world-2017, accessed October 2, 2017.

Chapter 4

1 Erica Frantz and Natasha Ezrow, *The Politics of Dictatorship: Institutions and Outcomes in Authoritarian Regimes* (Boulder, CO: Lynne Rienner, 2011).

2   "Idi Amin," *The Scotsman*, August 18, 2003, http://www.
scotsman.com/news/obituaries/idi-amin-1-660737, accessed
October 23, 2017.

3   Samuel Decalo, "African Personalist Dictatorships," *Journal of
Modern African Studies* 23, no. 2 (1985): pp. 209–237.

4   Ibid.

5   Ludger Helms, *Comparing Political Leadership* (New York,
NY: Palgrave Macmillan, 2012), p. 8.

6   Robert Jervis, "Do Leaders Matter and How Would We Know?,"
Security Studies 22, no. 2 (2013): pp. 153–179.

7   Conroy-Krutz and Frantz, "Theories of Democratic Change
Phase II."

8   Frantz and Ezrow, *The Politics of Dictatorship*.

9   Ronald Wintrobe, *The Political Economy of Dictatorship*
(Cambridge, UK: Cambridge University Press, 1998).

10 "State Security Chief U Tong Chuk Promoted," *North Korea
Leadership Watch*, April 14, 2010, http://www.nkleadershipwatch.
org/2010/04/14/state-security-chief-u-tong-chuk-promoted/,
accessed May 3, 2018.

11 Simon Mundy, "Kim Jong Un Purge Suggests Struggle for
Loyalty in North Korea," *Financial Times*, May 14, 2015, https://
www.ft.com/content/690d17d6-fa15-11e4-b432-00144feab7de,
accessed May 3, 2018.

12 Natasha Ezrow and Erica Frantz, *Failed States and Institutional
Decay: Understanding Instability and Poverty in the Developing
World* (London, UK: Bloomsbury, 2014), p. 223.

13 Michael Bratton and Nicolas van de Walle, "Neo-Patrimonial
Regimes and Political Transitions in Africa," *World Politics* 46,
no. 4 (1994): pp. 453–489.

14 Ezrow and Frantz, *Failed States and Institutional Decay*,
pp. 192–193.

15 Storer H. Rowley, "If Hussein Is the 'Godfather,' Republican
Guard Is the 'Family,'" *Chicago Tribune*, January 27, 1991, http://
articles.chicagotribune.com/1991-01-27/news/9101080595_1_
guard-divisions-guard-units-republican-guard, accessed October
23, 2017.

16 Barbara Geddes, "Minimum-Winning Coalitions and
Personalization of Rule in Authoritarian Regimes," paper
presented at the American Political Science Association Annual
Meeting, Chicago, IL (2004).

17 Milan Svolik, *The Politics of Authoritarian Rule* (Cambridge, UK: Cambridge University Press, 2012).

18 Andrea Kendall-Taylor, Erica Frantz, and Joseph Wright, "The Global Rise of Personalized Politics: It's Not Just Dictators," *Washington Quarterly* 40, no. 1 (2017): pp. 7–19.

19 Ibid.

20 Ibid.

21 Jeremy Brown, "Terrible Honeymoon: Struggling with the Problem of Terror in Early 1950s China," May 1, 2010, https://ucsdmodernchinesehistory.wordpress.com/2010/05/01/1045/, accessed October 23, 2017.

22 Michael Forsythe, "Q. and A.: Carl Minzer on the Shift to Personalized Rule in China," *The New York Times,* May 24, 2016, https://www.nytimes.com/2016/05/25/world/asia/china-carl-minzner-xi-jinping.html, accessed October 23, 2017.

23 Geddes, "Minimum-Winning Coalitions and Personalization of Rule in Authoritarian Regimes."

24 Svolik, *The Politics of Authoritarian Rule.*

25 The first comes from Geddes, "Minimum-Winning Coalitions and Personalization of Rule in Authoritarian Regimes"; the last five come from Kendall-Taylor, Frantz, and Wright, "The Global Rise of Personalized Politics."

26 Geddes, "Minimum-Winning Coalitions and Personalization of Rule in Authoritarian Regimes."

27 Fiona Hill and Cliff Gaddy, *Mr. Putin: Operative in the Kremlin* (Washington, DC: Brookings Institute Press, 2013).

28 Benedict Mander, "Venezuela: Up in Smoke," *Financial Times,* September 16, 2012, https://www.ft.com/content/e0cdedba-fe4e-11e1-8228-00144feabdc0, accessed October 24, 2017.

29 Paul Kirby, "Turkey Coup Attempt: Who's the Target of Erdogan's Purge," *BBC News,* July 20, 2016, http://www.bbc.com/news/world-europe-36835340, accessed October 24, 2017.

30 Kevin Woods, James Lacey, and Williamson Murray, "Saddam's Delusions: The View from the Inside," *Foreign Affairs* 85, no. 3 (2006).

31 Steve Douglas, "Referendum: Hitler's 'Democratic' Weapon to Forge Dictatorship," *Executive Intelligence Review* 4, no. 14 (2005); Frederick T. Birchall, "Hitler Endorsed by 9 to 1 in Poll on His Dictatorship, but Opposition Is Doubled," *The New York Times,* August 19, 1934.

32 Stephen Kurczy, "5 Reasons Why Haiti's Jean-Claude Duvalier Is Infamous," *Christian Science Monitor,* January 20, 2011, https:// www.csmonitor.com/World/Americas/2011/0120/5-reasons-why-Haiti-s-Jean-Claude-Duvalier-is-infamous/Tonton-Macoutes, accessed October 24, 2017.

33 Kendall-Taylor, Frantz, and Wright, "The Global Rise of Personalized Politics."

34 Eric Chang and Miriam A. Golden, "Sources of Corruption in Authoritarian Regimes," *Social Science Quarterly* 91, no. 1 (2010): pp. 1–20.

35 Jessica L. Weeks, "Strongmen and Straw Men: Authoritarian Regimes and the Initiation of International Conflict," *American Political Science Review* 106, no. 2 (2012): pp. 326–347.

36 Christopher Way and Jessica L. Weeks, "Making It Personal: Regime Type and Nuclear Proliferation," *American Journal of Political Science* 58, no. 3 (2014): pp. 705–719.

37 Frantz and Ezrow, *The Politics of Dictatorship.*

38 Michaela Mattes and Mariana Rodriguez, "Autocracies and International Cooperation," *International Studies Quarterly* 58, no. 3 (2014): pp. 527–538.

39 Joseph Wright, "How Foreign Aid Can Foster Democratization in Authoritarian Regimes," *American Journal of Political Science* 53, no. 3 (2009): pp. 552–571.

40 Geddes, Wright, and Frantz, "Autocratic Breakdown and Regime Transitions."

41 These categories come from Andrea Kendall-Taylor and Erica Frantz, "How Autocracies Fall," *Washington Quarterly* 37, no. 1 (2014): pp. 35–47. The data on authoritarian leader exits used in this book come from Svolik, *The Politics of Authoritarian Rule.* They cover the years 1950 to 2008. Data for the years 2009 to 2012 come from updates by Kendall-Taylor and Frantz in "How Autocracies Fall."

42 This term comes from Hein Goemans, Kristian Gleditsch, and Giacomo Chiozza, "Introducing Archigos: A Data Set of Political Leaders," *Journal of Peace Research* 46, no. 2 (2009): pp. 269–283.

43 Floriana Fossato, "Russia: Analysis—Reasons Behind Yeltsin's Resignation," RadioFreeEurope/RadioLiberty, December 9, 1999, https://www.rferl.org/a/1093002.html, accessed October 27, 2017.

44 Kendall-Taylor and Frantz, "How Autocracies Fall."

45 Nikolay Marinov and Hein Goemans, "Coups and Democracy," *British Journal of Political Science* 44, no. 4 (2013): pp. 799–825.

46 Kendall-Taylor and Frantz, "How Autocracies Fall."

47 Mohamed Nagdy and Max Roser, "Civil Wars," *Our World in Data*, 2016, https://ourworldindata.org/civil-wars/, accessed October 27, 2017.

48 Kendall-Taylor and Frantz, "How Autocracies Fall."

49 Data on leader fate used in this book come from Hein Goemans, Kristian Gleditsch, and Giacomo Chiozza, "Introducing Archigos." The most recent year these data are available is 2004.

50 William Taubman, *Krushchev: The Man and His Era* (New York, NY: W.W. Norton, 2003).

51 Abel Escriba-Folch and Joseph Wright, "Human Rights Prosecutions and Autocratic Survival," *International Organization* 69, no. 2 (2015): p. 354.

52 For a summary, see Erica Frantz, Andrea Kendall-Taylor, and Natasha Ezrow, "Autocratic Fate: How Leaders' Post-Tenure Expectations Influence the Behavior of Dictatorships," *Whitehead Journal of International Diplomacy* 15, no. 1 (2014): pp. 1–17.

53 Alexandre Debs and Hein E. Goemans, "Regime Type, the Fate of Leaders, and War," *American Political Science Review* 104, no. 3 (2010): pp. 430–445; Giacomo Chiozza and Hein E. Goemans, *Leaders and International Conflict* (Cambridge, UK: Cambridge Press, 2011).

54 Weeks, "Strongmen and Straw Men."

55 Library of Congress, "Uganda: A Country Study" (Washington, DC: Federal Research Division, 1992); Herman Lupogo, "Tanzania: Civil-Military Relations and Political Stability," *African Security Review* 10, no. 1 (2001): pp. 75–86.

56 Abel Escriba-Folch, "Repression, Political Threats, and Survival under Autocracy," *International Political Science Review* 34, no. 5 (2013): pp. 543–560.

57 Geddes, Wright, and Frantz, "Autocratic Breakdown and Regime Transitions."

58 Ibid.

59 Barbara Geddes, *Paradigms and Sand Castles* (Ann Arbor: University of Michigan Press, 2003).

60 Andrea Kendall-Taylor and Erica Frantz, "When Dictators Die," *Journal of Democracy* 27, no. 4 (2016): pp. 159–171.

Chapter 5

1   "Robert Mugabe Could Contest Election as Corpse, Says Wife," *The Guardian*, February 17, 2017, https://www.theguardian.com/world/2017/feb/17/robert-mugabe-could-contest-election-as-corpse-says-wife, accessed October 30, 2017.

2   "Zimbabwe," *Transparency International*, https://www.transparency.org/country/ZWE, accessed October 30, 2017.

3   "Botswana's Ian Khama to Step Down Next Year," *The East African*, March 21, 2017, http://www.theeastafrican.co.ke/news/Botswana-Ian-Khama-step-down-next-year/2558-3858598-sv90m6/index.html, accessed October 30, 2017.

4   "Botswana," *Transparency International*, https://www.transparency.org/country/BWA, accessed October 30, 2017.

5   "New Man, New Discipline," *Africa Confidential*, April 11, 2008, https://www.africa-confidential.com/article-preview/id/2541/New_man%2c_new_discipline, accessed October 30, 2017.

6   "Botswana," *Freedom House*, 2017, https://freedomhouse.org/report/freedom-world/2017/Botswana, accessed October 30, 2017.

7   Data on political parties and legislatures used in this book come from Jose Antonio Cheibub, Jennifer Gandhi, and James Raymond Vreeland, "Democracy and Dictatorship Revisited." The most recent year these data are available is 2008. Data on elections used in this book come from the NELDA data set [see Susan D. Hyde and Nikolay Marinov, "Which Elections Can Be Lost?" *Political Analysis* 20, no. 2 (2012): pp. 191–210]. The most recent year these data are available is 2010.

8   For an extensive discussion of these tactics and their purpose, see Erica Frantz and Lee Morgenbesser, " 'Smarter' Authoritarianism: The Survival Tools of Dictators," paper presented at the Southern Political Science Association Annual Meeting, New Orleans, LA (2017).

9   Kendall-Taylor and Frantz, "Mimicking Democracy."

10   Ezrow and Frantz, "Dictators and Dictatorships."

11   Ibid.

12   Larry J. Diamond, "Thinking About Hybrid Regimes," *Journal of Democracy* 13, no. 2 (2002): pp. 21–35.

13   Steven Levitsky and Lucan A. Way, "The Rise of Competitive Authoritarianism," *Journal of Democracy* 13, no. 2 (2002): pp. 5–21.

14   Andreas Schedler (ed.), *Electoral Authoritarianism: The Dynamics of Unfree Competition* (Boulder, CO: Lynne Rienner, 2006).

15 "Political Regime Characteristics and Transitions, 1800–2010," *Polity IV,* 2010, http://www.systemicpeace.org/polity/polity4. htm, accessed November 2, 2017.

16 "Freedom in the World 2017," *Freedom House,* 2017, http://www. freedomhouse.org/report/freedom-world/freedom-world-2014, accessed November 2, 2017.

17 Natasha Ezrow, "Hybrid Regimes," in *The SAGE Encyclopedia of Political Behavior,* edited by Fathali M. Moghaddam (Thousand Oaks, CA: SAGE, 2017), pp. 366–370.

18 Diamond, "Thinking About Hybrid Regimes," p. 28.

19 Wintrobe, *The Political Economy of Dictatorship;* Stephen Haber, "Authoritarian Government," in *The Oxford Handbook of Political Economy,* edited by Barry Weingast and Donland Wittman (Oxford, UK: Oxford University Press, 2006), pp. 693–707.

20 Geddes, Wright, and Frantz, "Autocratic Breakdown and Regime Transitions"; Michael Wahman, Jan Teorell, and Axel Hadenius, "Authoritarian Regime Types Revisited: Updated Data in Comparative Perspective," *Contemporary Politics* 19, no. 1 (2013): pp. 19–34; Jose Antonio Cheibub, Jennifer Gandhi, and James Raymond Vreeland, "Democracy and Dictatorship Revisited," *Public Choice* 143, no. 1–2 (2010): pp. 67–101.

21 Frantz, "Autocracy."

22 Cheibub, Gandhi, and Vreeland, "Democracy and Dictatorship Revisited"; Steffen Kailitz, "Classifying Political Regimes Revisited: Legitimation and Durability," *Democratization* 20, no. 1 (2013): pp. 39–60; Gustav Liden, "Theories of Dictatorships: Subtypes and Explanations," *Studies of Transition States and Societies* 6, no. 1 (2014): pp. 50–67; Wahman, Teorell, and Hadenius, "Authoritarian Regime Types Revisited."

23 Geddes, Wright, and Frantz, "Autocratic Breakdown and Regime Transitions."

24 Barbara Geddes, *Paradigms and Sand Castles: Theory Building and Research Design in Comparative Politics* (Ann Arbor: University of Michigan Press, 2003).

25 Ibid.; Michael Bratton and Nicolas Van de Walle, "Neopatrimonial Regimes and Political Transitions in Africa," *World Politics* 46, no. 4 (1994): pp. 453–489.

26 Peter B. Mayer, "Militarism and Development in Underdeveloped Societies," in *Encyclopedia of Violence, Peace and Conflict,* edited by Lester R. Kurtz and Jennifer E. Turpin (San Diego, CA: Academic Press, 1999), p. 434.

27 Barbara Geddes, Erica Frantz, and Joseph G. Wright, "Military Rule," *Annual Review of Political Science* 17, no. 1 (2014): pp. 147–162.

28 Geddes, *Paradigms and Sand Castles.*

29 Barbara Geddes, Joseph Wright, and Erica Frantz, *How Dictatorships Work* (New York, NY: Cambridge University Press, 2018).

30 Geddes, *Paradigms and Sand Castles.*

31 Blaine Harden, "Zaire's President Mobutu Sese Seko: Political Craftsman Worth Billions," *Washington Post*, November 10, 1987, p. A1.

32 Ezrow and Frantz, *Failed States and Institutional Decay.*

33 Geddes, Wright, and Frantz, "Autocratic Breakdown and Regime Transitions."

34 Ibid.

35 Weeks, "Strongmen and Straw Men."

36 Mark Peceny, Caroline C. Beer, and Shannon Sanchez-Terry, "Dictatorial Peace?" *American Political Science Review* 96, no. 2 (2001): pp. 15–26.

37 Way and Weeks, "Making It Personal."

38 Mattes and Rodriguez, "Autocracies and International Cooperation."

39 Abel Escriba-Folch and Joseph Wright, "Dealing with Tyranny: International Sanctions and the Survival of Authoritarian Rulers," *International Studies Quarterly* 54, no. 2 (2010): pp. 335–359.

40 Dan Reiter and Allan C. Stam, "Identifying the Culprit: Democracy, Dictatorship, and Dispute Initiation," *American Political Science Review* 97, no. 3 (2003): pp. 333–337.

41 Frantz and Ezrow, *The Politics of Dictatorship.*

42 Ibid.

43 Wright, "How Foreign Aid Can Foster Democratization in Authoritarian Regimes."

44 Joseph Wright, "Do Authoritarian Institutions Constrain? How Legislatures Affect Economic Growth and Investment," *American Journal of Political Science* 52, no. 2 (2008): pp. 322–343.

45 Chang and Golden, "Sources of Corruption in Authoritarian Regimes."

46 Geddes, *Paradigms and Sand Castles.*

47 Jay Ulfelder, "Contentious Collective Action and the Breakdown of Authoritarian Regimes," *International Political Science Review* 26, no. 3 (2005): pp. 311–334.

48 Christian Davenport, "State Repression and the Tyrannical Peace," *Journal of Peace Research* 44, no. 4 (2007): 485–504.

49 Hanne Fjelde, "Generals, Dictators, and Kings: Authoritarian Regimes and Civil Conflict, 1973–2004," *Conflict Management and Peace Science* 27, no. 3 (2010): pp. 195–218.

50 Leader duration and failure data come from Goemans, Gleditsch, and Chiozza, "Introducing Archigos."

51 Frantz and Ezrow, *The Politics of Dictatorship.*

52 Geddes, Wright, and Frantz, "Autocratic Breakdown and Regime Transitions."

53 The election in 2010 installed a civilian government in Myanmar and the election in 2015 gave the opposition a majority in both houses of the legislature. The military still remains very politically influential, however, so it is too soon (at the time of writing, at least) to assert that it has extricated itself from power.

54 Kendall-Taylor, Frantz, and Wright, "The Global Rise of Personalized Politics."

55 Ibid.

Chapter 6

1 Data on how authoritarian regimes seize power come from Geddes, Wright, and Frantz, *How Dictatorships Work*. Narratives of the seizure events draw from Geddes, Wright, and Frantz, "Autocratic Regimes Code Book, Version 1.2."

2 The breakdown of democracy in Venezuela was particularly slow and subtle. See Javier Corrales and Michael Penfold-Becerra, "Venezuela: Crowding Out the Opposition," *Journal of Democracy* 18, no. 2 (2007): pp. 99–113; Javier Corrales, "The Authoritarian Resurgence: Autocratic Legalism in Venezuela," *Journal of Democracy* 26, no. 2 (2015): pp. 37–51.

3 Geddes, Wright, and Frantz, *How Dictatorships Work.*

4 There has been little change since the end of the Cold War in the percentage of new dictatorships that sprouted at the time of a country's independence. This number is currently 22 percent, largely due to the breakup of the Soviet Union.

5 Ellen Lust and David Waldner, "Theories of Democratic Change Phase I: Unwelcome Change: Understanding, Evaluation, and Extending Theories of Democratic Backsliding," USAID, June 11, 2015, https://www.iie.org/Research-and-Insights/Publications, p. 67.

6   Ibid.

7   "How Poland's Government Is Weakening Democracy," *The Economist*, July 25, 2017, https://www.economist.com/blogs/ economist-explains/2017/07/economist-explains-25, accessed November 13, 2017.

8   Joshua Keating, "European Countries Are Backsliding on Democracy, and the EU Is Powerless to Stop Them," January 13, 2016, http://www.slate.com/blogs/the_slatest/2016/01/ 13/poland_is_backsliding_on_democracy_and_the_eu_is_ powerless_to_stop_it.html, accessed November 13, 2017.

9   "Freedom in the World 2017: Poland," *Freedom House*, 2017, https://freedomhouse.org/report/freedom-world/2017/ Poland, accessed November 13, 2017.

10   Steven A. Cook, "How Erdogan Made Turkey Authoritarian Again," *The Atlantic*, July 21, 2016, https://www.theatlantic. com/international/archive/2016/07/how-erdogan-made- turkey-authoritarian-again/492374/, accessed November 13, 2017.

11   "Venezuela: Chavez Allies Pack Supreme Court," *Human Rights Watch*, December 13, 2004, https://www.hrw.org/news/2004/ 12/13/venezuela-chavez-allies-pack-supreme-court, accessed November 14, 2017.

12   "Closing Doors? The Narrowing of Democratic Space in Burundi," *Human Rights Watch*, November 23, 2010, https:// www.hrw.org/report/2010/11/23/closing-doors/narrowing- democratic-space-burundi, accessed November 14, 2017.

13   "Elections in Benin," *African Elections Database*, http:// africanelections.tripod.com/bj.html, accessed November 14, 2017.

14   "Zambia: Elections and Human Rights in the Third Republic," *Human Rights Watch*, 1996, https://www.hrw.org/reports/1996/ Zambia.htm, accessed November 14, 2017.

15   Henri Barkey, "Turkey Will Never Be the Same after This Vote," *The Washington Post*, April 11, 2017, https://www. washingtonpost.com/news/democracy-post/wp/2017/ 04/11/turkey-will-never-be-the-same-after-this-vote/?utm_ term=.0351f82436d7, accessed November 14, 2017.

16   "Turkey Referendum: Erdogan Wins Vote amid Dispute over Ballots—As It Happened," *The Guardian*, April 17, 2017, https://www.theguardian.com/world/live/2017/apr/16/

turkey-referendum-recep-tayyip-erdogan-votes-presidential-powers, accessed November 14, 2017.

17 Erica Frantz, "Democracy Dismantled: Why the Populist Threat Is Real and Serious," *World Politics Review,* March 14, 2017, https://www.worldpoliticsreview.com/articles/21516/democracy-dismantled-why-the-populist-threat-is-real-and-serious, accessed November 13, 2017.

18 Geddes, Wright, and Frantz, "Autocratic Regimes Code Book," Version 1.2.

19 Geddes, Wright, and Frantz, *How Dictatorships Work.*

20 Andrea Kendall-Taylor and Erica Frantz, "How Democracies Fall Apart: Why Populism Is a Pathway to Autocracy," *Foreign Affairs,* December 5, 2016, https://www.foreignaffairs.com/articles/2016-12-05/how-democracies-fall-apart, accessed November 13, 2017.

21 Ibid.

22 Robert D. Crassweller, *Peron and the Enigmas of Argentina* (New York, NY: W. W. Norton, 1987), p. 222.

23 "World Summit in Quotes," *BBC News,* September 4, 2002, http://news.bbc.co.uk/2/hi/africa/2231001.stm, accessed November 14, 2017.

24 Rex A. Hudson, "The 1990 Campaign and Elections," *Peru: A Country Study* (Washington, DC: Library of Congress, 1992).

25 "Anti-Corruption Crusader Wins Belarus Vote: Runoff: Alexander Lukashenko Is Elected in a Landslide. He Will Be the Former Soviet Republic's First President," *Los Angeles Times,* July 11, 1994, http://articles.latimes.com/1994-07-11/news/mn-14295_1_alexander-lukashenko, accessed November 14, 2017.

26 "Is 'Populist International' Undermining Western Democracy?," *Democracy Digest,* November 7, 2016, https://www.demdigest.org/populism-undermining-western-democracy/, accessed November 14, 2017.

27 Kendall-Taylor and Frantz, "How Democracies Fall Apart."

28 Florence Peschke, "Journalists Still under Pressure in Duterte's Philippines," *International Press Institute,* February 10, 2017, https://ipi.media/journalists-still-under-pressure-in-dutertes-philippines/, accessed November 15, 2017.

29 Richard Javad Heydarian, "Rodrigo Duterte's Path to Dictatorship in the Philippines," *The National Interest,* June 1, 2017, http://nationalinterest.org/blog/the-buzz/

rodrigo-dutertes-path-dictatorship-the-philippines-20952,
accessed November 15, 2017.

30 Kim Lane Scheppele, "Hungary: An Election in Question," *The New York Times*, February 28, 2014, https://krugman.blogs. nytimes.com/2014/02/28/hungary-an-election-in-question-part-1/, accessed November 15, 2017.

31 Eszter Zalan, "Journalists Furious as Hungary's Largest Newspaper Closes," *EU Observer*, October 10, 2016, https:// euobserver.com/political/135416, accessed November 15, 2017.

32 "Hungary: Freedom in the World 2017," *Freedom House*, 2017, https://freedomhouse.org/report/freedom-world/2017/ hungary, accessed November 15, 2017.

33 "Nicaragua: Freedom in the World 2017," *Freedom House*, 2017, https://freedomhouse.org/report/freedom-world/2017/ Nicaragua, accessed November 15, 2017.

34 Cas Mudde, "The Problem with Populism," *The Guardian*, February 17, 2015, https://www.theguardian.com/ commentisfree/2015/feb/17/problem-populism-syriza-podemos-dark-side-europe, accessed November 14, 2017.

35 Kendall-Taylor and Frantz, "How Democracies Fall Apart."

36 Ibid.

Chapter 7

1 Wintrobe, *The Political Economy of Dictatorship*.

2 Niccolo Machiavelli, *The Prince*, translated by George Bull (London, UK: Penguin Books, [1514] 1995), p. 8.

3 Johannes Gerschewski, "The Three Pillars of Stability: Legitimation, Repression, and Co-optation in Autocratic Regimes," *Democratization* 20, no. 1 (2013): pp. 13–38.

4 Christian Davenport, "State Repression and Political Order," *Annual Review of Political Science* 10, no. 1 (2007): p. 2.

5 Steven Poe and Neal Tate, "Repression of Human Rights to Personal Integrity in the 1980s: A Global Analysis," *American Political Science Review* 88, no. 4 (1994): pp. 853–872.

6 Neil MacFarquhar, "Saddam Hussein, Defiant Dictator Who Rules Iraq With Violence and Fear, Dies," *The New York Times*, December 30, 2006, http://www.nytimes.com/2006/12/30/ world/middleeast/30saddam.html, accessed November 17, 2007.

7 Ezer Vierba, "Panama's Stolen Archive," *NACLA*, https:// nacla.org/article/panama's-stolen-archive, accessed November 17, 2017.

8   Lucan A. Way and Steven Levitsky, "The Dynamics of Autocratic Coercion After the Cold War," *Communist and Post-Communist Studies* 39, no. 1 (2006): pp. 387–410.

9   Stathis Kalyvas, *The Logic of Violence in Civil Wars* (Cambridge, UK: Cambridge University Press, 2006); Mark Irving Lichbach, "Deterrence or Escalation? The Puzzle of Aggregate Studies of Repression and Dissent," *Journal of Conflict Resolution* 31, no. 2 (1987): pp. 266–297.

10 Way and Levitsky, "The Dynamics of Autocratic Coercion After the Cold War."

11 Ibid., p. 392.

12 Christopher J. Fariss, "Respect for Human Rights Has Improved Over Time: Modeling the Changing Standard of Accountability in Human Rights Documents," *American Political Science Review* 108, no. 2 (2014): 297–318.

13 Christian Davenport, "State Repression and the Tyrannical Peace," *Journal of Peace Research* 44, no. 4 (2007): pp. 485–504.

14 See, respectively, Mark Gibney, Linda Cornett, Reed Wood, Peter Haschke, and Daniel Arnon, "The Political Terror Scale 1976–2015," 2016, http://www.politicalterrorscale.org, accessed November 17, 2017; and David L. Cingranelli, David L. Richards, and K. Chad Clay, "The CIRI Human Rights Dataset," 2014, http://www.humanrightsdata.com, accessed November 17, 2017.

15 Davenport, "State Repression and the Tyrannical Peace."

16 Ibid.

17 "Freedom in the World 2010. Methodology," *Freedom House*, 2010, http://www.freedomhouse.org/report/freedom--world-2010/methodology, accessed November 17, 2017.

18 Erica Frantz and Andrea Kendall-Taylor, "A Dictator's Toolkit: Understanding How Co-optation Affects Repression in Autocracies," *Journal of Peace Research* 51, no. 3 (2014): pp. 332–346.

19 Davenport, "State Repression and the Tyrannical Peace."

20 Ibid.

21 Ibid., p. 17.

22 Abel Escriba-Folch, "Repression, Political Threats, and Survival Under Autocracy," *International Political Science Review* 34, no. 5 (2013): 543–560.

23 The examples discussed here come from Frantz and Morgenbesser, "'Smarter' Authoritarianism."

24 George Ayittey, *Defeating Dictators: Fighting Tyranny in Africa and Around the World* (New York, NY: Palgrave Macmillan, 2011).

25 Kelley Bryan and Howard Rubin, "The Misuse of Bankruptcy Law in Singapore," *Lawyers' Rights Watch Canada,* 2012, http://www.lrwc.org/ws/wp-content/uploads/2012/03/MisuseOfBankruptcyLaw.pdf, accessed November 26, 2017.

26 "Ugandan Government Deployed FinFisher Spyware to 'Crush' Opposition, Track Elected Officials and Media in Secret Operation during Post-Election Protests, Documents Reveal," *Privacy International,* 2015, https://www.privacyinternational.org/node/657, accessed November 26, 2017.

27 Gregory Maus, "Eye in the Skynet: How Regimes Can Quell Social Movements Before They Begin," *Foreign Affairs,* July 1, 2015, https://www.foreignaffairs.com/articles/china/2015-07-01/eye-skynet, accessed November 26, 2017.

28 Fariss, "Respect for Human Rights Has Improved Over Time."

29 Jeff Corntassel, "Partnership in Action? Indigenous Political Mobilization and Co-optation During the First UN Indigenous Decade (1995–2004)," *Human Rights Quarterly* 29, no. 1 (2007): pp. 137–166.

30 Andrei Shleifer and Daniel Treisman, *Without a Map: Political Tactics and Economic Reform in Russia* (Cambridge, MA: MIT Press, 2000), p. 8.

31 Wintrobe, *The Political Economy of Dictatorship.*

32 Beatriz Magaloni and Ruth Kricheli, "Political Order and One-Party Rule," *Annual Review of Political Science* 13, no. 1 (2010): pp. 123–143.

33 Timur Kuran, "Now Out of Never: The Element of Surprise in the East European Revolution of 1989," *World Politics* 44, no. 1 (1991): pp. 7–48.

34 Frantz and Kendall-Taylor, "A Dictator's Toolkit."

35 Beatriz Magaloni, "Credible Power-Sharing and the Longevity of Authoritarian Rule," *Comparative Political Studies* 41, no. 4–5 (2008): pp. 715–741.

36 Magaloni and Kricheli, "Political Order and One-Party Rule."

37 Beatriz Magaloni, *Voting for Autocracy* (New York, NY: Cambridge University Press, 2006).

38 Jennifer Gandhi and Adam Przeworski, "Authoritarian Institutions and the Survival of Autocrats," *Comparative Political Studies* 40, no. 11 (2007): pp. 1279–1301.

39   Jennifer Gandhi, *Political Institutions Under Dictatorship* (Cambridge, UK: Cambridge University Press, 2008).

40   Jennifer Gandhi and Ellen Lust-Okar, "Elections Under Authoritarianism," *Annual Review of Political Science* 12, no. 1 (2009): pp. 403–422.

41   Ellen Lust-Okar, *Structuring Conflict in the Arab World: Incumbents, Opponents, and Institutions* (New York, NY: Cambridge University Press, 2005).

42   Yuen Yuen Ang, "Co-optation & Clientelism: Nested Distributive Politics in China's Single-Party Dictatorship," *Studies in Comparative International Development* 51, no. 3 (2016): pp. 235–256.

43   David Rock, *Argentina, 1516–1987: From Spanish Colonization to Alfonsín* (Berkeley, CA: University of California Press, 1987), p. 371.

44   Valery Lazarev and Paul Gregory, "Commissars and Cars: A Case Study in the Political Economy of Dictatorship," *Journal of Comparative Economics* 31, no. 1 (2003): pp. 1–19.

45   Magaloni, *Voting for Autocracy*, p. 47.

46   While the selectorate theory has implications for patterns of co-optation—it predicts that leaders of regimes with winning coalitions that are smaller relative to the size of the selectorate will be able to "buy" the loyalty of coalition members at a lower price—it is difficult to apply the theory to authoritarian contexts and therefore not discussed here. For the selectorate theory, see Bueno de Mesquita, Smith, Siverson, and Morrow, *The Logic of Political Survival*. For an in-depth critique of the theory's application to authoritarian environments, see Mary E. Gallagher and Jonathan K. Hanson, "Power Tool or Dull Blade? Selectorate Theory for Autocracies," *Annual Review of Political Science* 18, no. 1 (2015): pp. 367–385.

47   Benjamin Smith, "Life of the Party: The Origins of Regime Breakdown and Persistence under Single-Party Rule," *World Politics* 57, no. 3 (2005): p. 447.

48   Ezrow and Frantz, *Dictators and Dictatorships*.

49   Abel Escriba-Folch and Joseph Wright, "Dealing with Tyranny: International Sanctions and the Survival of Authoritarian Rulers," *International Studies Quarterly* 54, no. 2 (2010): 335–359.

50   Jake Maxwell Watts and Nopparat Chaichalearmmongkol, "In Thailand, a Struggle for Control of State Firms," *The Wall*

Street Journal, June 17, 2014, https://www.wsj.com/articles/
in-thailand-a-struggle-for-control-of-state-firms-1402930180,
accessed November 28, 2017.

51 Lex Rieffel, "State-Owned Enterprises and the Future of the
Myanmar Economy," *The Brookings Institution*, September 16,
2015, https://www.brookings.edu/blog/up-front/2015/09/
16/state-owned-enterprises-and-the-future-of-the-myanmar-
economy/, accessed November 28, 2012.

52 Kristina Mani, "Military Entrepreneurs: Patterns in Latin
America," *Latin American Politics and Society* 53, no. 3 (2011): p. 25.

53 Ezrow and Frantz, *Dictators and Dictatorships*.

54 Andrew Nathan, "Authoritarian Resilience," *Journal of Democracy*
14, no. 1 (2003), p. 14.

55 Magaloni and Kricheli, "Political Order and One-Party Rule,"
p. 128.

56 Magaloni, *Voting for Autocracy*.

57 Barbara Geddes, "What Do We Know About Democratization
After Twenty Years?" *Annual Review of Political Science* 2, no. 1
(1999): p. 129.

58 See Frantz, "Autocracy."

59 Thomas Pepinsky, "The Institutional Turn in Comparative
Authoritarianism," *British Journal of Political Science* 44, no. 3
(2014): 631–653.

60 Frantz and Morgenbesser, " 'Smarter' Authoritarianism."

61 William Dobson, *The Dictator's Learning Curve: Inside the Global
Battle for Democracy* (New York, NY: Doubleday, 2012), pp. 23–24.

62 Samuel A. Greene, *Moscow in Movement: Power and Opposition in
Putin's Russia* (Palo Alto, CA: Stanford University Press, 2014),
p. 103.

63 Frantz and Morgenbesser, " 'Smarter' Authoritarianism."

64 Alexander Cooley, "Countering Democratic Norms," *Journal of
Democracy* 26, no. 3 (2015): pp. 49–63.

65 Sohrab Ahmari and Nasser Weddady, *Arab Spring Dreams: The
Next Generation Speaks Out for Freedom and Justice from North Africa
to Iran* (New York, NY: Macmillan, 2012), p. 161.

66 Kendall-Taylor and Frantz, "Mimicking Democracy to Prolong
Autocracies."

67 Gandhi, *Political Institutions Under Dictatorship*.

68 Frantz and Kendall-Taylor, "A Dictator's Toolkit."

69 Dobson, *The Dictator's Learning Curve*, p. 121.

70   Erica Frantz and Andrea Kendall-Taylor, "The Evolution of Autocracy: Why Authoritarianism Is Becoming More Formidable," *Survival* 59, no. 5 (2017): pp. 57–68.

71   Kendall-Taylor and Frantz, "Mimicking Democracy to Prolong Autocracies." The authoritarian regime data are available starting in 1946, but the start year here is 1951 to enable computation of whether a regime held an election in the last six years.

72   Frantz and Morgenbesser, " 'Smarter' Authoritarianism."

Chapter 8

1   Data on how authoritarian regimes collapse come from Geddes, Wright, and Frantz, *How Dictatorships Work*, and my updates of this data set. Narratives of the failure events draw from Geddes, Wright, and Frantz, "Autocratic Regimes Code Book," Version 1.2.

2   Henry Lubega, "Amin's Downfall Begins After 20 Months in Power," *Daily Monitor*, January 16, 2017, http://www.monitor. co.ug/Magazines/PeoplePower/Amin-s-downfall-begins-after-30-months-in-power/689844-3517058-qvd3fuz/index.html, accessed November 30, 2017.

3   In the data set used here, elections are not considered regime-change events if authoritarian incumbents win them, even if they are relatively free and fair.

4   Mark A. Uhlig, "Turnover in Nicaragua; Nicaraguan Opposition Routs Sandinistas; U.S. Pledges Aid, Tied to Orderly Turnover," *The New York Times*, February 27, 1990, http:// www.nytimes.com/1990/02/27/world/turnover-nicaragua-nicaraguan-opposition-routs-sandinistas-us-pledges-aid-tied. html?pagewanted=all, accessed November 30, 2017.

5   Anti-government revolt data come from Erica Chenoweth and Orion Lewis, "Unpacking Nonviolent Campaigns: Introducing the NAVCO 2.0 Dataset," *Journal of Peace Research* 50, no. 3 (2013): pp. 415–423.

6   "Somalia Profile—Timeline," *BBC News*, September 4, 2017, http://www.bbc.com/news/world-africa-14094632, accessed November 30, 2017.

7   Maureen Covell, *Madagascar: Politics, Economics and Society* (London, UK: Francis Pinter, 1987).

8   Kendall-Taylor and Frantz, "How Autocracies Fall."

9   Jonathan M. Powell and Clayton L. Thyne, "Global Instances of Coup from 1950 to 2010: A New Dataset," *Journal of Peace Research* 48, no. 2: p. 252.

10 Coup data (available for the 1950 to 2010 period) come from
    Powell and Thyne, "Global Instances of Coup from 1950 to 2010."

11 Deniz Aksoy, David B. Carter, and Joseph Wright, "Terrorism in
    Dictatorships," *Journal of Politics* 74, no. 3 (2012): pp. 810–826.

12 These ideas come from Geddes, *Paradigms and Sand Castles.*

13 Ibid., p. 131.

14 Ibid., p. 130.

15 See Conroy-Krutz and Frantz, "Theories of Democratic Change
    Phase II," for an exhaustive review of the literature covering
    these factors.

16 Przeworski, Alvarez, Cheibub, and Limongi, *Democracy and
    Development.*

17 Geddes, Wright, and Frantz, "How Dictatorships Work."

18 Magaloni, *Voting for Autocracy.*

19 Joseph Wright, Erica Frantz, and Barbara Geddes, "Oil and
    Autocratic Regime Survival," *British Journal of Political Science* 45,
    no. 2 (2015): pp. 287–306.

20 Mauricio Rivera Celestino and Kristian Skrede Gleditsch, "Fresh
    Carnations or All Thorn, No Rose? Nonviolent Campaigns and
    Transitions in Autocracies," *Journal of Peace Research* 50, no. 3
    (2013): pp. 385–400.

21 Geddes, Wright, and Frantz, "Autocratic Breakdown."

22 Ibid.

23 Though this trend may give rise to optimism for proponents
    of global democracy, it should be noted that in recent years
    democracies are being replaced by dictatorships almost as
    frequently as they are replacing them, as discussed in
    Chapter 1.

24 Rivera Celestino and Skrede Gleditsch, "Fresh Carnations or All
    Thorn, No Rose?"

25 See Conroy-Krutz and Frantz, "Theories of Democratic Change
    Phase II," for an in-depth discussion of these issues.

26 Hans Lueders and Ellen Lust, "Multiple Measurements, Elusive
    Agreement, And Unstable Outcomes in the Study of Regime
    Change," *V-Dem Institute Working Paper,* September 2017,
    https://papers.ssrn.com/sol3/papers.cfm?abstract_id=3042470,
    accessed December 1, 2017.

27 Log Raditlhokwa, "Botswana: Dictatorship in a Democracy,"
    AllAfrica, August 8, 2004, http://allafrica.com/stories/
    200408091208.html, accessed November 30, 2017; Nicola de Jager,
    "Why Elections in Botswana and South Africa Can Be 'Free'

But Not 'Fair,' " *Democracy in Africa,* January 14, 2014, http://democracyinafrica.org/elections-bostwana-south-africa-can-free-fair/, accessed December 1, 2017.

28   Lueders and Lust, "Multiple Measurements."

29   These ideas draw from Conroy-Krutz and Frantz, "Theories of Democratic Change Phase II."

30   Ibid., p. 6.

31   See, for example, Andreas Schedler, *The Politics of Uncertainty: Sustaining and Subverting Electoral Authoritarianism* (Oxford, UK: Oxford University Press, 2013); Gandhi, *Political Institutions Under Dictatorships;* Grigore Pop-Eleches and Graeme B. Robertson, "Information, Elections, and Political Change," *Comparative Politics* 47, no. 4 (2015): pp. 459–495.

32   Marian Gallenkamp, "Democracy in Bhutan: An Analysis of Constitutional Change in Buddhist Monarch," *Institute of Peace and Conflict Studies,* March 2010, http://www.ipcs.org/pdf_file/issue/RP24-Marian-Bhutan.pdf, accessed December 1, 2017.

33   Mark Farmaner, "This Burma Is a Democracy Now? Think Again," *The World Post,* November 8, 2015, https://www.huffingtonpost.com/mark-farmaner/burma-election-democracy_b_8505384.html, accessed December 1, 2017; Max Fisher, "Myanmar, Once a Hope for Democracy, Is Now a Study in How It Fails," *The New York Times,* October 19, 2017, https://www.nytimes.com/2017/10/19/world/asia/myanmar-democracy-rohingya.html?_r=0, accessed December 1, 2017.

34   Kendall-Taylor and Frantz, "Mimicking Democracy to Prolong Autocracies."

35   Daniela Donno, "Elections and Democratization in Authoritarian Regimes," *American Journal of Political Science* 57, no. 3 (2013): pp. 703–716.

36   Geddes, Wright, and Frantz, "Autocratic Breakdown."

37   Geddes, *Paradigms and Sand Castles.*

38   "Burkina General Says Ex-president Compaore Not Linked to Coup," *Reuters,* September 17, 2015, https://www.yahoo.com/news/burkina-general-says-ex-president-compaore-not-linked-151309050.html, accessed December 2, 2017.

39   Paul Collier, "In Praise of the Coup," *New Humanist,* March 4, 2009, https://newhumanist.org.uk/articles/1997/in-praise-of-the-coup, accessed December 2, 2017.

40 George Derpanopoulos, Erica Frantz, Barbara Geddes, and Joseph Wright, "Are Coups Good for Democracy?" *Research and Politics* 3, no. 1 (2016): pp. 1–7.

41 Michael L. Ross, "Does Oil Hinder Democracy?," *World Politics* 53, no. 3 (2001): pp. 321–365.

42 Stephen Haber and Victor Menaldo, "Do Natural Resources Fuel Authoritarianism? A Reappraisal of the Resource Curse," *American Political Science Review* 105, no. 1 (2011): pp. 1–26.

43 Wright, Frantz, and Geddes, "Oil and Autocratic Regime Survival."

44 Eleanor Albert, "What to Know About the Sanctions on North Korea," *Council on Foreign Relations,* November 27, 2017, https://www.cfr.org/backgrounder/what-know-about-sanctions-north-korea, accessed December 3, 2017.

45 Hossen G. Askari, John Forrer, Hildy Teegen, and Jiawen Yang, *Economic Sanctions: Explaining Their Philosophy and Efficacy* (Westport, CT: Praeger, 2003).

46 Abel Escriba-Folch and Joseph Wright, "Dealing with Tyranny: International Sanctions and the Survival of Authoritarian Rulers," *International Studies Quarterly* 54, no. 2 (2010), pp. 335–359.

47 Christian von Soest and Michael Wahman, "Are Democratic Sanctions Really Counterproductive?," *Democratization* 22, no. 6 (2015): pp. 957–980.

48 Stephen D. Collins, "Democracy Sanctions: An Assessment of Economic Sanctions as an Instrument of Democracy Promotion," *Taiwan Journal of Democracy* 5, no. 2 (2009): pp. 69–96.

49 Simone Dietrich and Joseph Wright, "Foreign Aid and Democratic Development in Africa," in *Democratic Trajectories in Africa: Unraveling the Impact of Foreign Aid,* edited by Danielle Resnick and Nicolas van de Walle (Oxford, UK: Oxford University Press, 2013), p. 57.

50 See Conroy-Krutz and Frantz, "Theories of Democratic Change Phase II," for a review of this literature.

51 Abel Escriba-Folch and Joseph Wright, *Foreign Pressure and the Politics of Autocratic Survival* (Oxford, UK: Oxford University Press, 2015).

52 Steven E. Finkel, Anibal Perez-Linan, and Mitchell A. Seligson, "The Effects of U.S. Foreign Assistance on Democracy Building, 1990–2003," *World Politics* 59, no. 3 (2007): pp. 404–440.

53   Ibid.

54   Simone Dietrich and Joseph Wright, "Foreign Aid Allocation Tactics and Democratic Change in Africa," *Journal of Politics* 77, no. 1 (2014): pp. 216–234.

55   Rivera Celestino and Skrede Gleditsch, "Fresh Carnations or All Thorn, No Rose?"

56   "How Filipino People Power Toppled Dictator Marcos," *BBC News*, February 17, 2016, http://www.bbc.com/news/av/magazine-35526200/how-filipino-people-power-toppled-dictator-marcos, accessed December 4, 2017.

57   Peter Ackerman and Jack DuVall, *A Force More Powerful: A Century of Non-Violent Conflict* (New York, NY: Palgrave Macmillan, 2000), p. 384.

Chapter 9

1   Geddes, Wright, and Frantz, *How Dictatorships Work.*

2   Milan Svolik, "Which Democracies Will Last? Coups, Incumbent Takeovers, and the Dynamic of Democratic Consolidation," *British Journal of Political Science* 45, no. 4 (2014): pp. 715–738.

3   See, for example, Mark J. Gasiorowski and Timothy J. Power, "The Structural Determinants of Democratic Consolidation: Evidence from the Third World," *Comparative Political Studies* 31, no. 6 (1998): pp. 740–771.

INDEX